If History Is Our Guide

J.C. Phillips

For My Wife and My Mother

Contents

Introduction 2

2011 4

Citizen Murdoch: A Case for Treason 5

The Republican Party: The Party of Big Government 6

It's Ok To Get High: The Drug Users Union 8

Egypt: From Protest to Revolution 10

The Tea Party is the new White Citizen Council 12

Neo-McCarthyism 13

Marijuana Makes You Crazy!! 14

Japan: A Lesson From America 16

Stopping Genocide 18

Raped In Libya 19

Remembering Marvin Gaye 20

Seems Like Old Times 21

Two Schools Of Thought 22

Lessons Not Learned 25

It's the End of the World...Again 26

Closure 28

Death to Trickle-Down Economics! 29

Introducing the Viagra Condom 30

The End of the World Didn't Happen... Now What? 31

A Message for the Class of 2011 32

Learning Democracy 101 34

Jim Crow All Over Again 35

Stop!! No Saggy Pants Allowed 36

Shut Up and Vote!! 37

Michael Jackson Remembered 38

The Malcontents: Volume 1 39

The Malcontents: Volume 2 41

Check Out My Index Finger!!! 43

Carpe Diem 43

The Empire Strikes Back 45

An Artist Remembered: Amy Winehouse 48

Happy Birthday, Mr. President 48

What Happened to Sean Hoare? 51

Blame Yourself America!! 52

Armageddon...Take 2 53

Remembering Hurricane Katrina 54

Muammar Hearts Leezza 57

Can Ecstasy Cure Cancer? 58

9/11: A Retrospective 58

To Serve with Pride 59

Japan: Six Months Later 60

99 Percent 61

What Were Steve Jobs' Last Words? 62

Occupy 64

Vindication 69

Scary Things 71

What Were Steve Jobs Last Words? : Volume 2 72

In Memory of Andy Rooney 73

WATCH OUT!!! You Almost Stepped In That. 73

The Empire Strikes Back: Volume 2 74

Giving Thanks 76

Stocking Stuffer! 77

Occupy Equals Financiers 77

An Offer for Robert Reich 78

My Christmas Wish 80

Is Common Sense Back In Vogue?...81

2012 82

The Clowns Are In Town!! 83

Advice for the Returning Veteran..85

We're Sorry Dr. King 87

25 Books That Shaped America 90

Random Acts of Kindness 92

Jim Crow All Over Again: The America's Cup..............................92

The Great Migration Back to the South.......................................95

The Importance of the Separation of Church and State 96

War Fatigue 97

Limbaugh's Fluke 98

What The Fuck Is Up With Gas Prices?..99

The Inevitable Scandal..100

Strip Search Everyone...101

Nazis In Congress 102

The Great Student Loan Debt Debate 102

In Yo' Face (book), Saverin 103

Defend New Orleans: Volume 2 104

Eliminate Student Debt 107

Happy Birthday America..110

It's Official... No One Likes Mitt Romney 112

The End of Racism 113

Defend New Orleans: Volume 3 114

A Review of the Republican National Convention......................116

A Review of the Democratic National Convention 117

Good Luck India 119

Voting Against Your Own Self Interest 121

For What It's Worth..122

For What It's Worth: Volume 2 124

Review of the Last Presidential Debate.. 124

Common Sense Prevails 125

Mitt Hearts G.O.P 126

Giving Thanks: Volume 2 128

A Family Affair 129

2013 130

Respect 131

Good Riddance...112th Congress... 131

The Way Forward 132

The Importance of Black History Month 134

The Blame Game 135

The Mental Health Issue.. 136

Rupert Murdoch's Phone-Hacking Scandal- What's Happened? 139

The Trouble with Donations and NPO's 140

Like Father, Like Son 141

Senseless 142

Skyfall 144

Comfortable In His Own Skin.. 145

Advice for the Class of 2013 146

Spy Games 147

How to Stop a Dictator from Becoming a Dictator................................. 148

The End of Racism: Volume 2 149

Here We Go Again: The Looming Budget Battle 150

Farewell Letter to Mahmoud Ahmadinejad 152

Stop and Frisk: Ruled Unconstitutional 153

A Savvy Political Stroke.. 153

You Lost...Get Over It... 155

Seems Like Old Times: Volume 2.. 156

So It Begins- The Holiday Season 157

Giving Thanks: Volume 3 157

Let Us Ponder For a Moment 158

A Christmas Wish: Volume 2 159

2014 160

2014 Mantra: I Quit!!! 161

America's New Slavery System: Prison 161

Let Them Have Cake: The FIFA World Cup 162

The Mayans Were Almost Right 164

Not Again!!! 164

The End of Racism: Volume 3 166

Problems or Solutions 168

What the Hell Happened In August? 171

What is Domestic Violence? 171

This is the Beginning of the End 173

For What It's Worth: Volume 3 176

Scary Things. Volume 2 177

Coming Soon....U.S. Government Shutdown 2015 179

Hope 180

2015 183

The Ghost of David Duke 184

#RupertsFault 187

Beware of that MOJO 188

WATCH OUT!!! You Almost Stepped In That: Volume 2 189

The Cancer Event 190

Social Terrorist 190

A Stagnant Economy 191

About Baltimore 194

The Week that Changed America 196

Goodbye Rupert 199

Epilogue 200

Bibliography 202

Introduction

In 2011 when I first wrote 1lovejoy blog I wanted to chronicle the presidency of Barack Obama and to write about the social and political landscape shaping the world. Needless to say my point of view changed as time went on. I saw agendas being waged, and some of those agendas were selfish and mean spirited. Then this blog became something more... a calling if you will. I stated my blog mission statement with this manifesto;

> "This blog is to serve notice to all extreme elements in our society that they are being watched. From the far left to the far right, they will not be spared from the orgy of common sense that is sure to come from this blog.
>
> For far too long, the people in the middle (moderates) have been told by the extreme voices in our society which way to think about the political, religious, and social issues. For far too long, the extreme voices in our society led us to war and religious regression.
>
> But, now it is time for common sense. What I mean by common sense is that the only prevailing stand will be the right one that brings all positions together. As long as societies exist, compromise is the key to keep these societies going. If History is to be our guide, no extreme society lasts. The only society that strives is the society that is an educated one. Through education we can make an educated decision and learn from the history of our human experience.
>
> I will pledge to you that this blog will only reflect a mirror on society. I will present issues that will come from a place where education and history will guide my blog.
>
> This blog is to fight ignorance and discuss real issues that affect real people. No spin, no agenda, just the truth from a moderate point of view."

This was the goal of the blog- to have people think about the issues facing our world with common sense and not use emotion to justify a certain position.

This book is a chronicle of the best and worst elements of the human struggle. I hope this book will make you laugh, cry and remember the atmosphere of when these events took place.

The American poet Robert Frost once said, "*In three words I can sum up everything I've learned about life: it goes on.*" Maybe there's something in those words that is comforting and scary, but we must face the challenges head on to find solutions to our own problems so we can find solutions to the bigger ones.

2011

"You see things; and you say "Why?" But I dream things that never were; and I say "Why not?"

– George Bernard Shaw

Citizen Murdoch: A Case for Treason

Rupert Murdoch is an Australian-born billionaire who owns a number of conservative media outlets around the globe to manipulate his neoconservative point of view. Most notably in the United States is his Fox Network empire. Lax media regulation in America has enabled his News Corporation Group to control the political debate to his favor.

Mr. Murdoch publishes 175 newspapers (notably The New York Post and Wall Street Journal), and controls 40% of the United States media via his Fox Empire and local television stations. This man is slowly but surely taking and shaping his agenda via these various outlets. In India, they view Mr. Murdoch's past business behavior and neoconservative views as such a threat that if he sets foot on the sub-continent he will be arrested immediately. I believe the United States should follow India's lead.

To put it simply, Mr. Murdoch is a union buster; tax evader; war monger; neoconservative oil imperialist; Bush Supporter and employer; New York City political boss and a human rights violator. The frightening part is that this is not even half of what he has done. The labels that are placed upon him are easily documented and proof that Mr. Murdoch should be tried for treason or expelled from the United States.

The political discourse has been in free fall since the advent of Fox News. The attitude of Us vs. Them (whites and the others) is a disgusting display of neoconservative self-promotion. Moreover, the vile display of American sunshine patriotism is a slap in the face to all the men and women who served their country (myself included). He is an affront and should be stopped.

Rupert Murdoch's actions have caused me to look in the mirror and question, "What has America Become?" I realized after the election of President Obama that America was tired of fighting. America just wanted things done. My hope was restored, that my America, rejected the neo-conservatism agenda for at least 4 years.

On a personal note, I hate what the Murdoch agenda has done to my country. I hate the way he uses his media empire to manipulate common fears. I hate that he promotes mindless racists and bigots by giving them an arena to voice their opinions. His news media group does not report the news, they report his opinions. He is a modern day Randolph Hearst, a yellow journalist. Citizen Murdoch, leave my beloved country alone and go back to the land down under. You are damaging America. Enough!!!!

January 31st

The Republican Party: The Party of Big Government

Ever since I can remember, the Republican Party always accused the Democratic Party of being a bunch of 'tax and spend liberals'. This strategy continues to serve the Republican Party well to this day. However, those in the know can rebuke this agreement to its core. If you are a conservative, you may want to take a seat before you continue to read this.

Since the advent of the 20th century, almost all Republican administrations have expanded the role of government. By expanding the role of government, they raise the national debt to unparalleled proportions. Most people are under the illusion that Republicans reduce the role of government in our lives. However, I beg to differ because I have history and economics on my side.

First, The Reagan Administration ran the deficit up to its highest level by putting all the money into defense spending and cutting taxes for wealthy Americans and Corporations. He called this theory "Trickle Down Economics". This theory states that the very rich will give the economy a boost to provide for the rest of us poor souls. Needless to say that history proved this theory a disaster. In 1980 when George H.W. Bush (41st) was running as a Presidential Candidate for the Republican Party (he later became Ronald Reagan's Vice President) he said that "Trickle Down Economics" was "Voodoo Economics". How prophetic those words had become because on October 19th 1987, the stock market crashed (the day was soon to be called "Black Monday"). It took two years for the economy to recover. Consequently, George H.W. Bush became the 41st President of the United States and followed the same "Voodoo Economics" his predecessor had created. However, it was those same principles that cost him the 1992 Presidential Election.

In 2000, President Clinton's Administration cleaned up all the damage that the Reagan-Bush Administration did to the American economy. The Clinton Administration used common sense and cut wasteful spending in all government departments. This truly was the age of a leaner government that the Republicans always preached about but was carried out by a Democrat. The U.S economy hadn't had a surplus since President Andrew Jackson (the seventh President of the United States, a Democrat).

The economic future looked bright until the flawed election of George W. Bush (43rd). He inherited a surplus and he spent it just as fast as he could on 2 wars; expansion of more government agencies; tax cuts and a bunch of tireless wasteful spending. And before you knew it, we had another record deficit that exceeded the Reagan-Bush Administration combined. Moreover, Bush 43rd Administration failed to do what was necessary to stop the "Great Recession". In addition, Bush 43rd administration enjoyed a majority Republican Congress that approved all of his budgets with no questions asked.

Recently, the American people elected a Democrat (President Barack Obama) to get us out of the mess that we allowed another Republican Administration to get away with. When will the American electorate learn that the real party of 'tax and spend' is the G.O.P. and not the Democrats? As history as a guide, it does not look good for the Republican Party. And I didn't even mention the S&L bailout involving the Bush Family when Bush 41 was President.

The current Republican Party is good on several issues- fighting the culture wars, starting wars, lowering taxes for the very wealthy and corporations, misinformation of facts, and raising the national debt. In a nut shell, that is the Republican Party. And we, the American Public are to be blamed. When things are good we elect a Republican but when things go shitty we elect a Democrat to get us out of our economic fix. We demand more from

Democrats than from the other party in a shorter time. This is totally unfair at every level.

Haven't we learned anything about the Republicans/Conservatives? They care about their bottom line. They will use whatever tactics they deem necessary to control power and get over on the little guy. Republican/Conservatives believe in the "Free Market". They do not care if you suffer or get hurt. Wake up America and realize that Republicans/Conservatives think that you are "Suckers".

February 1st

It's Ok To Get High: The Drug Users Union

There's a saying that goes, "The road to hell is paved with the best intentions". This is what I thought when I saw a report about a new Union calling themselves "The Drug Users Union". The creation of such a Union proposal amused me but to my disbelief there were already established "Drug Users Unions" in New York, San Francisco, Canada, and Europe! Apparently, this union believes that drug users have an image problem and would like to clean up the image of drugs and drug users. Once again, let me explain the folly of this Union and why people will not take it seriously as a force for change.

I did a little research to check out the "Drug Users" unions' mission statement. Basically it states that they want, "to decriminalize drugs and drug use; to create a safe environment where people can use & enjoy drugs as well as receive services; to promote a positive image of drug users to engender respect within our community and from outside our community; to work towards access to better quality and safer drugs; to ensure fair treatment by the law, by service providers, and by health care workers; and to advocate for more harm reduction-based services including counseling and overdose prevention."

I agree with the premise that these unions want to provide counseling and overdose prevention. However, on a television interview, Simon Perez (a news reporter out of San Francisco), stated that the Unions said (Para-phasing), "We figure people are going to do drugs anyway. We just want them to have a safe place to do it." Not once in the report did they mention offering meaningful alternative programs to try to get people into rehab programs. Ms. Alexandra Goldman (Coordinator in San Francisco) stated that "We (the Union) have a non-judgmental attitude about drug use."

Besides the occasional recreational drug users, from what I've seen, most abusers of drugs are homeless, mentally ill or physically and psychologically abused people. By giving them a place to use drugs is almost criminal. These Unions are harboring an environment where drug users and dealers will have a place to make their transactions simpler. And I worry that the Union hall will become like a crack house.

Let's face it, the so-called "War on Drugs" is not working. As long as people have stress and peer pressure in their lives, drug uses will still be a problem. Moreover, as long as politicians (in the United States) need a theme to run for offices, drugs will remain illegal. All of the lobbying efforts in the world will not help this cause. There are too many governmental agencies (DEA, FBI, HLS, etc.) that need drug prevention money to round out their annual budgets.

The only countries that have a grasp of the situation are Amsterdam and Portugal. In these countries government action puts drug users and sellers in certain designated areas to root out trouble before it begins and also brings in needed revenue (mostly from tourists). As a result, research shows that drug use has gone down in these countries.

"The Drug User's Unions" may have the best intentions but I fear that people will take advantage of their mission. I wonder if this Union was started by some trust fund babies that thought it was a cool idea to get high all day and start a group with people who also like getting high. Let's face it most NGO's are started by Ivy League, financially and politically connected groups who are disconnected from reality. I know it sounds a little harsh, but after reading the mission statement and doing the research, their goal seems a bit fuzzy (no pun intended).

Egypt: From Protest to Revolution

The British statesman and philosopher, Edmund Burke once said, "Those who don't know history are destined to repeat it". With the ever changing events in Egypt, it appears that the Egyptian military will take over the country just like the military coup in Pakistan during the late 1970's. Or maybe some elements of the 'Muslim Brotherhood' will seize control (Iranian Revolution, 1979). Both scenarios seem to be the reality each and every day this chaos continues. The West also feels the economic and military investment put toward Egypt will be all for naught.

For example, Pakistan in 1977 went through a military coup where they arrested Zulfikar Ali Bhutto and his cabinet under the orders of General Zia - who was Head of the Pakistan military at the time. Zia called for new elections, released Bhutto only to re-arrest him twice (for fear he may be elected again). Eventually, Bhutto was executed. Zia then postponed the election because he said, "that he changed his decision due to the strong public demand for the scrutiny of political leaders who had engaged in malpractice in the past." As soon as Bhutto was executed, Zia maneuvered his way to become President/Dictator of Pakistan. This could be the same scenario that Egypt is facing.

To make matters worse we are seeing the advent of the new group who call themselves 'The Coalition' which includes the 'Muslim Brotherhood'. This scares the western powers because the 'Muslim Brotherhood' is a branch of Al-Qaeda. Al-Qaeda's second in command was in the 'Muslim Brotherhood' before joining Al-Qaeda. Now that 'The Coalition' is involved in this revolution, this can only mean that Muslim extremist will have another haven to direct operations. This is bad news for Saudi Arabia, Jordan and Israel.

Historically, Pakistani and Iranian revolutions have set in motion regimes of religious/theocratic rule. Most people believe that if we (the West) lose Egypt as an ally, then the Middle East will fall like a house of cards to Muslim extremist groups, just as it did in Iran (Iranian Revolution, 1979). The very thought of having another Iran on our hands is beyond comprehension. Another reason why Egypt is so important to the West is because it keeps the peace between Arab nations. Moreover, it protects Israel from being attacked by other Arab nations - especially Iran. The West relies on Egypt for their back door diplomatic communications with the rest of the Middle East. The West needs Egypt to be stable and reliable at all cost. Too much time, money, and resources have been put toward making Egypt the most important political player in the region.

The United States government has an awful track record of supporting heavy handed dictators because we like stable relationships for business agendas. Moreover, Egypt is in a very strategic position with the Suez Canal bringing oil from Saudi Arabia to Europe and the rest of the world. Not to mention the vital role it plays in military logistics. Commerce has freely flowed through this canal from all around the world and the only time the Suez Canal was closed was from 1967 to 1975. This canal and by default Egypt is the life-line to the Western economy whether you like it or not.

The downside of this business arrangement is that these same leaders fail to provide basic necessities like food, clothing, jobs, and basic services for their people. As long as we don't see the injustice, we are content to go along with the program. However, when these same leaders need a whipping boy to blame, the West becomes a scapegoat (namely the United States, France and Great Britain). In the eyes of their people, we are to blame for their suffering. And of course the West will take it all in stride in order to do business.

The West worries that revolutionary protest in the Middle East always turns out to be chaotic no matter how good the intentions may be. Let's face facts, this is a leaderless movement. With no leadership, this is sure to be a fiasco. The U.S. has to walk a fine line because we talk about how democracy is the greatest form of government in the world but we do not like the choice of whom the people select -remember Palestine. Under these circumstances "What should America do?" Watch and hope that the Egyptian people get what they truly want, a real democracy.

The Tea Party is the new White Citizen Council

February is Black History Month in the United States. PBS (Public Broadcast System) usually shows the ground breaking documentary series called 'Eyes on the Prize'. This documentary gives an account of the Civil Rights Movement during the mid-1950's until the 1980's for the fight for equality in the United States. While watching this documentary, I was shocked to hear about the 'White Citizen Council (WCC)'. The WCC was an organization that was started in the Deep South to keep segregation intact and to preserve the (white) southern way of life. Any notion of integration would be fought by any means necessary. The language and the violent tone in their words and actions struck me in an odd and familiar way. The same rhetoric, tone and violence are used by the 'Tea Party' movement. The 'Tea Party' movement feels that their way of life is threatened and the only way to stop the oncoming tide of change is to resist by all means.

Even before the election of President Obama, there was a ground swell for this sort of movement to exist. In the documentary by Alexandra Pelosi, 'Right America; Feeling Wronged-Some Voices from the Campaign Trail', she followed the McCain /Palin campaign trail to give a forum to conservative voices. The people who were interviewed sounded just like the members of the WCC and at the end of the documentary when they knew they were going to lose, their frustrations were unleashed. Their political rallies looked more like Klu Klux Klan meetings. It wasn't the fact that they were going to lose this election, it was the fact that a person of color was to be President of the United States.

The 'Tea Party' movement, just like the WCC, is using resistance in the form of political and legal maneuvering which impedes an economic recovery. This is evident when most legislative bills that come from the White House are questioned and mauled over. And you better believe that the 'Tea Party' and their allies, Fox News and Conservative radio, is going to hold the administrations feet to the fire. The whole collective has no real agenda to get U.S. out of trouble. Their whole movement is obstructionist. Just like the WCC was.

Let just call a spade a spade. The 'Tea Party' movement just like the WCC is a bunch of racists, bigots, and obstructionist who love nothing more than to see our President fail. This is their thinking. They wish that the country will fail just out of racist spite. Don't they know that the Civil War is over? Hey 'Tea Party' members, you lost. Move on and get over the fact that your President is a Black man. Get over the fact that people of color are more than capable of running the country. Get over the fact that your children may fall in love with a person of color. Get over the fact that your good ole' days are over. In order to survive in today's society one must be open to new ideas and a new way of thinking. Your hate will eat you alive.

February 15th

Neo-McCarthyism

"McCarthyism" in Webster's New Collegiate Dictionary is defined as: "a mid-twentieth-century political attitude characterized chiefly by opposition to elements held to be subversive and by the use of tactics involving personal attacks on individuals by means of widely publicized indiscriminate allegations esp. on the basis of unsubstantiated charges." For years, the Republican Party (U.S.) used this method to structure the political conversation, but now it has perfected this to an art form. The new waves of this neo–McCarthyism are: - Fox News and The Tea Party.

Fox News is the quintessential headquarter for this neo-McCarthyism movement. This 24 hours cable news channel presents the news in the most bias unabashed way. Conservative rhetoric is spun as real news. The cast of characters that host their most popular shows are more like runaways from an insane asylum. Bill O'Reilly, Glenn Beck, and their colleagues offer slanted information in the most fear-mongering way imaginable. Approval for this kind of yellow journalism comes from the puppet master that is running the whole show - Rupert Murdoch- the Australian billionaire that brought his brand of neo-conservatism to the United States.

The 'Tea Party' is the new voice for neo-McCarthyism and is made up of Conservatives and Libertarians, who want to limit government spending, reduce government and the federal deficient as well as national debt. But in reality, the party (Republicans) that they align themselves with did the exact same thing in all so-called conservative administrations. This is evident in the revelation that Bush 43$^{rd's}$ administration squandered the budget surplus that was handed at the end of the Clinton administration. These known truths make the 'Tea Party' movement a farce as they pick and choose their concern about the economy and the state of the country. Why is it that during 8 years of the Bush 43rd administration nothing was being done by these so-called 'Tea Party' members but now that there is a Democrat in the White House the national debt suddenly is an issue again?

If you look at the rallies and gatherings it appears that this Neo-McCarthyism movement is brought on by mostly Caucasians who are afraid that people of color will take over the government and change the American way of life(whatever that is). After the election of President Obama, the whole neo–conservative movement has proven to become obstructionist. They use personal attacks, indiscriminate allegations and unsubstantiated charges to make the American public fearful. This is classic McCarthyism 101. For example, most 'Tea Party' rallies displayed slogans and posters using racial slurs and misinformation about Mr. Obama's and his proposals for the American people. One infamous poster attacking the Health Care legislation proposal read "Witch Doctor", showing the President in so-called Witch doctor apparel with a bone in his nose. This kind of scene harkens back to the days of the Civil Rights movement in which Dr. Martin Luther King Jr. was called a "Communist" and a "Socialist" and racial slurs were hurled at him.

This neo-conservative/neo-McCarthyism movement is all about keeping and maintaining control of a 'certain' way of life. Don't let them win. Don't let fear win.

February 17th

Marijuana Makes You Crazy!!

In the United States, there is a movement to make cannabis legal. The measure that would allow people to legally purchase, sell and smoke the substance. Most people consider marijuana to be a harmless herb and compare its use to drinking a beer or a cocktail but with medicinal properties. However, there is a new study that suggests otherwise.

According to a recent study, marijuana is linked to psychosis. In other words, smoking marijuana can cause schizophrenia. The research was a review of 83 studies and with over 22,000 participants which showed that a person using Marijuana will develop some form of psychosis 2.7 years earlier than people who do not use cannabis at all. The review also shows that people who use illegal drugs suffer from psychosis two years earlier than persons who don't engage in that activity.

Matthew Large – a professor from The University of New South Wales is the author of the new research into cannabis called the "Archives of General Psychiatry". In this report they "provide evidence for a relationship between cannabis use and earlier onset of psychotic illness and they support the hypothesis that cannabis use plays a causal role in the development of psychosis in some patients." This research reinforces that people who use cannabis with a family history of psychosis are in grave danger. Maia Szalavitz of Time magazine "recently reported on a study that found that among 190 patients with schizophrenia, 121 of whom had used marijuana, cannabis appeared to affect the age of psychosis onset in a subgroup of 44 patients. The affected patients either had their first symptoms within a month of smoking pot for the first time, or experienced a severe worsening of psychotic symptoms each time they smoked."

People who have a family history of psychosis and take marijuana develop symptoms of schizophrenia faster than any other group who take the drug occasionally. That is a scientific fact. The new findings suggest that more focus should be placed on the long-term effects of someone who suffers from psychosis after using cannabis.

Most cannabis users take it to relax or take it for its medicinal properties but there are a lot of cannabis users that abuse this drug. Just like alcohol, the more one abuses it the more harm it will do. Marijuana is not a kid's drug and the people who support the legalization want to make people believe that it is harmless. Most people who are cannabis users will shrug off this study and call it tomfoolery but the fact of the matter is that the study proves that this drug is linked to psychosis. Get high now become crazy later. That doesn't sound like a good time.

March 15th

Japan: A Lesson From America

The Earthquake and Tsunami in Japan was truly shocking and the utter devastation in Japan (particularly Northern Japan) was of biblical proportions. While this is not the first earthquake/tsunami that caused destruction in our recent collective memories it is reminiscent of a hurricane that happened in 2005 - Hurricane Katrina.

Back in August 2005, when "Katrina" hit New Orleans, the city was spared the full force of the hurricane and it appeared that the "Big Easy" avoided another brush with destiny. However, the 9th Ward levy broke and all hell with it. The city was flooded out and the whole world watched and was helpless to do anything about it. Hurricane Katrina brought a city, a state, and the Bush 43rd Administration to its knees because all levels of government were unprepared for the sheer magnitude of the event. The world stood back and wondered why the world's most powerful nation would let their citizens die like animals. A stain on America's fabric was exposed.

Now, let us fast forward to the recent earthquake /tsunami in Japan. Again, the world stood by and watched the destruction caused by Mother Nature. Unlike America, the Japanese government and people were prepared for this event because they trained and drilled for this scenario. The Japanese people displayed their resolve in a trying situation. However, just like in the United States in 2005, transparency is not being fully disclosed. The elephant in the room is the nuclear power plants that are located around the country and the fact that the earthquake/tremors are causing havoc on the reactors is not a good sign.

Japan (just like the United States) is a strong and powerful country with a strong tradition of self-reliance but in light of the current situation this country needs help to prevent a nuclear meltdown. Masking the problem doesn't make it go away. The Bush 43 administration avoided the real issue that caused devastation in New Orleans. During and after Hurricane Katrina, Bush 43rd lost all credibility due to the lack of transparency and lack of compassion. This current crisis seems to be headed in the same direction.

Nuclear radiation affects not just an area but the world and being evasive is doing more harm than good. After Hurricane Katrina hit and the levy broke everyone was denying that help was needed and that the system was broken. Japan-this is your Katrina moment. Demand that the Prime Minister be more transparent with the world and the people of Japan about the danger of a possible nuclear meltdown. The world wants to help but only if you let us.

Kiyomizu Temple. Kyoto, Japan.

Stopping Genocide

In Africa there is a history of genocide. The examples that come to mind are Rwanda and Sudan. We watched as millions of people were slaughtered and we just sat on the sideline because we were conflicted in our need to protect our national interest- namely oil. These events could have been stopped if only we had used air power. Now we have that opportunity to right the wrong of the last decade.

The United States is leading the charge in Libya to enforce a "No Fly Zone" in that country. Some critics said too little too late and others want to know what the endgame is. We have to remember that the United States and other allies imposed a "No Fly Zone" in Iraq before the Bush 43rd Administration led the world to a misguided war. The "No Fly Zone" is the best solution because no troops (U.S.) will be involved in operations on the ground. President Obama has shown to be a very deliberate leader and instead of U.S. intervention in Egypt he chose back door negotiations with the Egyptian military to keep the peace. The strategy worked and now Egypt is plotting their course with little to no foreign intervention.

The same negotiation strategy was used in Libya but this didn't work with Gaddafi. When it appeared that the rebels would take control of Tripoli- Gaddafi's mercenary army fought back the rebels. The rebels asked the International community for air support so they can have a fair fight. Contrary to popular belief most Libyans believe that they can fight for their own country without foreign intervention.

Most reporters believe that the U.S. is in another war, but this is not the case. This mission is clear, take out the air and ground capability of Gaddafi's mercenary army; supply humanitarian aid for civilians and impose sanctions by the United Nation to force Gaddafi out of power. That is the Endgame.

The U.S. and the rest of the world are fatigued by war in the Middle East. The U.S. is about to end 2 ongoing wars by the end of 2011. The last thing the U.S. wants is to be involved in another conflict, but when there is an opportunity to stop genocide in some small way you jump at the opportunity. Just as President Clinton did in the Baltic- President Obama is doing in Libya. The moral responsibility is too great.

There will be no U.S. boots on the ground even though the media would have you believe that this is another war. The President made the United States role on this mission very clear. Unlike Bush 43rd - in President Obama I trust.

March 29th

Raped In Libya

The Webster New Collegiate Dictionary defines the word Rape as, "sexual intercourse with a woman by a man without her consent and chiefly by force or deception." On Saturday March 26th, a woman wanders into a Libyan Hotel (where foreign journalists are staying) and claims that she has been gang raped by fifteen men from the Gaddafi regime after being picked up at a Gaddafi militia checkpoint. She went on to say that she was held by the regime for two days while she was beaten and raped. She had the scars to prove it.

When the regime minders saw what was taking place they quickly shouted *Traitor* and tried to keep her from speaking to the press. One of the minders, sadly another woman, tried to put a table cloth over the victim's head. When foreign journalists tried to intervene they were shoved and pushed to keep away from the woman. The minders quickly put her in the car and sped away. The Gaddafi regime claimed she was intoxicated and that she is safe at home with her family. Journalists finally reached the family but were told that she has not returned.

This incident is a perfect example why the people want the Gaddafi regime ousted. It does make you wonder how many times women have been subjected to this sort of behavior? We will never truly know but we all bore witness to the courage this young Libyan woman displayed.

Remembering Marvin Gaye

On April 1ˢᵗ, 1984 a man tried to intervene in a physical altercation between his mother and father over business documents. For years the man's father physically abused his mother but now he was old enough to stop it. After it appeared that the altercation was over, in a blind rage his father went into his bedroom to retrieve a gun and then returned to shoot his son dead. 4 months earlier, that gun was a gift given by the son to his father. The next day on April 2ⁿᵈ the man would have turned 45 years old. That man was Marvin Gaye.

This was a tragic ending to a life and career that gave so many people joy. When the word of his death spread it felt like a family member passed away, especially for the Baby Boomers that grew up listening to his music and witnessing his evolution from sex symbol to musical legend.

The story of Marvin Gaye is a story of hope, loss, love and redemption. To know the Marvin Gaye story you must hear his music. Once you hear his words you will forever be changed by them and have a greater appreciation for the lessons he tries to teach. Here is the top five musical renderings you should hear by Marvin Gaye to hear why he is a legend.

1. Duets with Tammi Terrell- Most successful duet couple in the 1960's. They embodied the feel for the era. Songs like Your Precious Love, Ain't No Mountain High Enough, and Ain't Nothing like the Real Thing are just a few examples of this classic collaboration.

2. Midnight Love- This was Marvin's comeback album and it was awesome. The song Sexual Healing won him his first two and only Grammy.

3. Let's Get It On & Marvin Gaye Live- Classic Albums (notable songs are Let's Get It On & Distant Lover).

4. Here My Dear- This album takes a retrospective look at his relationship with his first wife and their painful divorce (notable song I Met a Little Girl).

5. What's Going On? - This album is Marvin Gaye's opus to the world. He talks about how rational human beings need to have an honest dialogue with one another to solve our problems.

For the life he led and the memories he gave us- Marvin Gaye is truly deserving of the title *Legend*. Happy Birthday!!

April 7th

Seems Like Old Times

In the mid-term elections of 1994, the American people elected a majority of Republicans to Congress. The Republicans had Newt Gingrich as their leader and they vowed to have a *Contract With America* to stop the agenda of President Clinton. They vowed to focus on the economy and get Americans back to work. However, as soon as they came into power the focus on the economy shifted to a focus on stopping Health Care Reform and in the process they managed to shut the government down for weeks. With these actions, the Republicans inadvertently saved President Clinton's presidency and ensured his re-election but unfortunately they also stopped Health Care Reform.

Let us fast forward to 2010, the American people elected a majority of Republicans to Congress. The Republicans have John Boehner as their leader and they vow that the *Tea Party* and the conservatives, if elected to Congress, will stop the agenda of President Obama. They vow to focus on the economy and get Americans back to work. Similar to 1996 the economy is not their concern but repealing Health Care Reform is their agenda and they are willing to shut down the federal government to get their way. If History is our guide then the Republicans are sure to fail in this endeavor. What they are doing is showing the American people their true character.

Whoever reads this blog knows that the neo-conservative moment is about creating fear. President Obama (just like President Clinton) will stand up to these fools and call their bluff. Just like in 1996, the Republican Party is conceding the presidential re-election to President Obama but unlike 1996 their efforts to stop Health Reform will fail.

It's amazing that the media and the public at large can fall for the same smoke and mirror routine that the Republican Party delivers year after year. Most educated people know that the Republican Party is made of wealthy individuals, who to maintain power manipulate on the fears of the uneducated, religious, patriotic and racist. As stated before, The Republican Party is playing the American public for suckers. 1996 and 2011, it seems like old times.

April 21st

Two Schools Of Thought

Looking at the state of the world indicates that we are at a transitional phase. On one hand you have the old guard that won't give up power without a fight and on the other hand you have a new generation who is telling the old guard that their time is over. The era of struggle is just beginning.

The Old Guard

The old guard is the Baby Boom generation. They fought for civil rights, voting rights, women rights, gay and lesbian rights; sexual freedom and voiced their opposition to the Vietnam War. Their inspiration was a young President (John F. Kennedy) and a young minister (Dr. Martin Luther King). With these men as inspirational leaders - they wanted to change the world and do things differently than the generation before them. To a degree they accomplished what they set out to do but in the process of becoming the old guard they reverted back to an old way of thinking. To maintain control they would throw around terms like *Family Values, Just Say No,* the *Moral Majority* and *Affirmative Action* to keep the masses in check. They replaced racial and gender bias with class warfare.

The Hippies became Yuppies and free love gave way to Wall Street and corruption. Talk shows; MTV; Reality TV and fast food were all the rage. They thought the party would last forever. To get a grasp of their generation you can look to the last two Presidents (Clinton & Bush 43). Both were ambitious and wanted to set their own agenda. These guys were still fighting the argument that they had in the 1960's about free markets and the moral and religious responsibility of a woman's right to choose and integration of minorities in the America fabric. It is an ideological battle that was left over from the days of Franklin Roosevelt's presidency - What is a government's responsibility to its people?

The New School

Generation X & Y is quickly taking over the role of leadership. With the election of President Obama we see that this generation is not afraid to take on the challenge. This generation is more traveled, more educated and have more diverse views than their predecessors. You can't label this group because on some issues they are conservative and on other issues liberal to moderate. One cannot pigeon hole this generation. Intellect, confidence and action are what they value. This generation heard the battle stories of the Baby Boomers and is respectful of their accomplishment but not satisfied about the outcome. Massive budget deficits; 2 wars; rogue nuclear weapons; hardline dictators; man-made and natural disasters, global meltdown, third world poverty; rising oil prices; terrorism; NAFTA, 401K Plans, Gay & Lesbian marriage, and rising Health Care and education problems or just a few unresolved issues that the old guard created for the new school.

The Problem

The new school has taken over but the old school is hovering around with their tried and true method of politics- fear. The perfect example of this brand of politics comes from the Bush 43rd administration with the lead up to the Iraq War. The talking points that were used were 9-11 and WMD (weapon of mass destruction) and it worked like a charm. The old school has been using this tactic for years and we still fall for it.

The new school method is transparency. The philosophy is, the more you know the more educated your decision. However, with the advent of the internet and broadband, we have a tendency of forming conspiracy theories and half-baked ideas about everything under the sun. With any invention if you put it in the hand of the wrong people chaos ensues. As the new school was raised in the 80's they expect everything to be done immediately and tend to forget that change is a process and not a microwave solution.

The Solution

The old school needs to take a step back and let the new school plot their own path. You can see it in the uprisings in the Middle East, North Africa, Africa, and Asia and with the elections of new leaders in Europe and America. The new school will not be denied their fundamental right to choose and will not be bullied by the old school powers. The old school tried and failed to secure economic freedom for their people. The old school forgot the principle that put them in office- to provide the people with basic needs to survive. Ideology doesn't put food on the table or provide shelter or creates jobs. Sensible leadership with a singular focus on those principles is what is needed.   Old school, you had your day in the sun but now it's time for a new brand of leadership. Step aside and let the new school get to work cleaning your mess.

The Martin Luther King, Jr. Memorial at Yerba Buena Gardens San Francisco, California

Lessons Not Learned

The American news media love to re-examine news stories 1 year later. Just recently the media is covering the events that took place in Haiti (earthquake); Chile (coal-miners cave collapse) and the Gulf Coast (oil spill). These stories had extended coverage that invoked people and governments to move quickly to solve the problems that arose at the time.

Who's to Blame?

We as human beings are caught up in the moment. We get upset or angry at the time and demand action. After some time has passed, we forget about the problem and go on with our everyday lives thanking the heavens that it's not us that is involved in that particular situation. Furthermore, we put the blame on the wrong people. The news media and the public at large love to put the blame on governments but the fact is that the problem should be placed on big corporations. The government didn't blow up the oil rig that spilled millions of gallons of oil into the Gulf of Mexico- BP did! The government didn't send those coal miners into harm's way- the coal industry in Chile did! However, the government in Haiti was and still is responsible for the response during aftermath of the earthquake. To this day the government of Haiti is allowing NGO's (Non- Government Organizations) to run the relief effort in Haiti (and they are failing miserably). It is the role of government to bring order to chaos. By no means should government shun its' citizens in time of need.

Keeping It Real

Let's be real for a moment, big corporations dictate what governments will and can do. Big corporations can provide jobs to communities and they have the power to take those jobs away. They also provide money for candidates seeking political office. That is the truth. Politicians need to cozy up to these companies to get jobs in their communities. If those politicians succeed they can go after the higher office they are seeking or become a lobbyist and join the big machine. Either way they are looking after their own best interest. This dance has been going on for years and whosoever gets in the way will be crushed.

In Conclusion

If we are true to ourselves we all know who is to blame- Big Corporations and our collective selves. Let's stop kidding ourselves- we use their computers, we drive their cars, we wear their clothes and shoes, we listen to their iPod, we watch their flat screen televisions, and we view their YouTube videos. We are all in the matrix and we are helpless to do anything about it. In a year's time we will re-examine what went wrong in Japan and we will come to the same conclusion. This is how the system works and we are happy to swallow the blue pill- like it or not.

April 28th

It's the End of the World...Again

In Oakland, California, billboards are popping up claiming that the world will apparently end on May 21, 2011. This claim is made by Harold Camping, the founder of a non-profit Christian Radio network which includes KEAR 610 AM in the Bay Area.

Mr. Camping claims on his website www.familyradio.com that there is evidence in the bible that the world will end on May 21st of this year. However, Mr. Camping made the same claim that the world was coming to an end in 1994.

So as not to be out done, an Atheist group is also putting up their own billboards countering Mr. Camping's claim. In fact, the group will hold a convention in Oakland on May 21st and will have a celebration party to mock Mr. Camping's claim of doom.

Canvasser handing out literature for Family Radio. UC Berkeley, California

Closure

The death of Osama Bin Laden is an opportunity to reflect on how much he affected our lives, especially here in America. He fundamentally changed the way we view people and religion, the way we travel, and the perception that the rest of the world has of America. Bin Laden achieved his goal by bringing chaos to what we took for granted in the west- this is what terrorism is all about.

Hope and Change

After 8 years of the *War on Terror* (Bush/Cheney War), we as Americans decided we wanted *Hope and Change*. We were tired of living in fear and decided to elect a young President with that same *Hope and Change* ideals we wanted the world to see. President Obama played down the rhetoric about the *War on Terror*. He simply ended an unpopular war in Iraq and focused on Afghanistan where we knew Osama Bin Laden might have been. The President applied pressure on Afghanistan and Pakistan to help catch this mass murderer. He also relied on the U.S. Military, human Intel, drones and Special Forces to collect enough evidence to get the job done and as a result Osama Bin Laden was eliminated. It took Mr. Obama's administration 2 years to complete this operation- it took the Bush/Cheney administration 8 years with no results and constant mishaps along the way.

Relief

All the sacrifice made by countless men and women around the globe doesn't feel in vain anymore. We were obsessed about catching Osama and it felt that the world was Captain Ahab chasing Moby Dick. Now we feel justified that a man who said that he would never be caught got shot between the eyes.

Reflection

The Webster's New Collegiate Dictionary defines *Terrorism* as, "*the systematic use of terror*". Killing Osama Bin Laden won't bring an end to terrorism but it delivered a message to would be terrorists that justice will be done no matter how long it takes. Each activity of terrorism brings heartache and pain to people who don't deserve it. And what makes it more pitiful is that they use religion as their rally cry – pathetic.

In Closing

If disagreements arise I hope we can take non-violent means to solve issues. It's ironic that the leader of Al-Qaeda was living it up in a mansion compound while his operatives are living like rats in caves and hovels. Osama Bin Laden was a rich kid playing revolutionary that disgraced a religion along the way. Bin Laden was a fraud. Let's turn the page on this terrible event in human history and focus on the healing process- I think we deserve that.

May 10th

Death to Trickle-Down Economics!

In the United States, it was always believed that if you were rich you paid more taxes. This has always been a staple of the American share value system. That value system is why the U.S. had the most stable market in the world. However, in the last 30 years the failed experiment with *trickle-down economics* has turned the American share value system upside down. Now it's believed that the more you make the less you get taxed and the less you make the more you get taxed-What? Did I miss something here? This is the reason why America is in a debt crisis.

A History Lesson

The late libertarian economist Milton Friedman came with the theory of supply-side economics *(trickle-down economics)*. The theory states that if you lower the tax rates for the rich that it would encourage more investment, which in turn will mean more jobs and higher tax revenue despite the lower tax rate. The man who championed this theory was

Ronald Reagan and when he became President in 1981 he turned the theory into action.

Protecting the Wealthy

The Wealthy in the United States do not pay their fair share and their champion is the Republican Party. In 2009, President Obama pushed for a tax cut to aid the working class. The name of the legislation is Making Work Pay Tax Credit. In order to pass the legislation, the Republicans who were poised to take control of Congress forced the President's hand into extending the Bush Era tax cuts for another 2 years. By doing so, the Republican held Congress raised taxes on a third of Americans that were considered the working poor. President Obama vowed never again to agree to an extension of the Bush Era tax cuts because of the Republicans double-crossing him on the agreed deal.

The Reality

Let's face facts, the wealthiest among us did not get wealthy because they were nice guys. These people work towards wealth, are married to wealth, inherited wealth, or were born into wealth and they will keep what they have until the very end. The words *conservative*, *free- market* and *capital gains* are code words for I'm rich and you're not and the phrase "*government regulation*" is an insult to their sensibilities. These people are selfish. The last 30 years has left a bigger gap between the have and have not's. This theory has eroded the social fabric of our society. Let us go back to the time where everyone paid their fair share and be forever done with this theory of supply-side economics because it is not working.

May 17th

Introducing the Viagra Condom

In the fight against erectile dysfunction, a British biotech firm Futura Medical (licensed to Durex), has introduced a condom called CSD500. The company claims that this product will help keep a man's erection longer and stronger-just like Viagra. The reason for this condom's staying power is vasodilating gel which helps blood flow to the penis to maintain a longer erection. This product is not meant for men with erectile dysfunction but rather for men who have trouble keeping their erection for long period of time. If this product takes off in Europe than the U.S. market is sure to follow. Apparently we can't find the cure for cancer but we can find a cure for a hard-on. Unbelievable!!

May 24th

The End of the World Didn't Happen... Now What?

On May 21st, at 6 pm, the world waited to see if Mr. Harold Camping's prediction about the end of days would come to pass. It did not!! We can all shake our collective head and laugh at the notion of Mr. Camping's failed prediction or we can examine his motives for making such a ridiculous claim.

Was It Money?

After all the articles written about Mr. Camping's end of day's prediction, no one thought to ask the question about how much money was given by families who believed in this guy? Can the people who followed Mr. Camping sue his organization *Family Radio*? No one asked about the families that sold all their personal belongings because of this man.

Was It Politics?

In 1994, Mr. Camping made the same prediction about the end of the world and we all know what happened. It seems that Mr. Camping makes these end of the world predictions whenever a Democrat is the President of the United States- 1994 President Clinton and 2011 President Obama. This is something to think about. In my opinion, I thought the world was going to end when George W. Bush was President-then he would have had me convinced.

Final Analysis

Mr. Camping is an 89 year old man with nothing to gain or lose with his prediction. What Mr. Camping does not realize is that people are affected by his words. Because he is the leader of a religious organization people tend to put a great deal of faith in his teaching. Mr. Camping has showed himself to be reckless with his prediction —not once but twice. In the New Testament, The book of Matthew 24:36 says, *"No one knows about that day or hour, not even the angels in heaven, nor the son, but only the father."* This particular passage should illustrate that no man knows when the end of the world will be-only God but I bet Mr. Camping and his followers missed that particular passage.

May 31st

A Message for the Class of 2011

To the graduating Class of 2011, I would like to leave you with some words of wisdom. These words come from my life experience. I hope you will gain knowledge from these lessons.

Be Daring - You have the whole world at your fingertips. At this point of your life you can choose your own path. The only person that is stopping you from achieving something is yourself. Life is about failure. Failure teaches us the most important life lessons; it's how we find our true character. Remember, life does not come with an instruction manual.

Travel - Traveling is the most important thing you can do. It takes you out of your comfort zone and what is familiar. Remember this, no place in the world is like the place you grew up in and people around the world are good and decent. The media will scare you about the outside world-don't listen and see for yourself.

Be Informed - Be aware of your surroundings. Reading your local newspaper and different periodicals around the world will give you different perspectives. Take it all in and make an informed decision.

Relationships - Your best friend in grammar school is probably not your best friend at this stage of your life and if they are that's great. But, for the majority of us that will not be the case; the truth of the matter is that people in your life change because people tend to change. Don't try to figure it out.

Taking Advantage - Older people tend to take advantage of youth- that has been the way of the world for centuries. But as a youth you'll have to find an older mentor or family member that you trust. Counsel from someone you trust will keep you from being taken advantage of.

Opportunity Knocks - When you get your shot at the big time- go for it! These are rare opportunities that come every once in a while. This is the time to throw caution to the wind and grab your opportunity when you can. Remember, people are successful when preparation meets opportunity.

Don't Be Reckless- Don't be reckless with someone's affection. Be honest and truthful with your feelings towards them. In the long run it will save you from any misunderstandings that should arise.

You Will Change - The older you get the more you will change. What was cool to do at 21 seems silly at age 24. Remember this, it's called maturity. It happens to the majority of us and some of us still need some growing up.

Patience - Things in life will not always go your way. You will face hardship. You will have people close to you pass away. You will have problems either professionally or personally. That's just life. If life taught me anything-it is to be patient. When things around you seem uncertain and chaotic, take a deep breath and analyze the situation. You're smart enough to work out your own problems and find a solution. Remember this, patience will service you well in times of trouble.

To the Class of 2011, I like to leave you with one principle to live by; *Respect those who respect you*. If you follow this simple principle you should do fine in your journey through life.

Learning Democracy 101

In the *Arab Spring* the ideology of Democracy is in bloom. People want the right to choose their own leaders by having free and fair elections. This is a philosophy that America cultivated throughout the world. However, the Arab world has failed to study how long a democracy takes to establish.

Recent History: Eastern Europe

Let's take a look back at the end of the *Cold War* and in particular the Eastern Block (now Eastern Europe). Back in the early 1990's it was a climate of hardline dictators, puppet governments and bad economy which led to the best and brightest leaving in droves and a bleak future. This is the same situation that's going on in the Middle East and North Africa as we speak. People in North Africa and the Middle East should look to the lessons of their counterparts in Eastern Europe and recognize that democracy is a long process. Democracy doesn't take weeks but years to establish.

Non-Violent Approach

Anyone can shoot a gun but the real power comes from non-violent means. Dr. Martin Luther King Jr. and Mahatma Gandhi taught the world the power of the human spirit. Note that the United States and India are the biggest democracies in the world and both are just now reaching the full potential of what a true democracy really means.

Facing Your Foes

If history is to be our guide, for any country to achieve a democratic form of government one has to have a foe. Eastern Europe- The former USSR, The U.S. and India-The British Empire, and now the Arab World –Hard-line dictators. Remember, freedom isn't free and the hardline dictators will not give up power without a fight and they are willing to retain power and will do anything to keep it. This struggle will build a national identity- embrace the challenge.

In Conclusion

Democracy is not a fast food form of government and things will not change overnight just because of wishful thinking. The people of the Middle East and North Africa have to pay the price for wanting a better life- no one can do it for them. It happened in America, India, and Eastern Europe. The world is pulling for you and is behind the *Arab Spring* all the way and if you succeed we will welcome you to the club.

June 9th

Jim Crow All Over Again

There is a story in *The New York Times* that has received little to no fanfare from the media. The article Voter Registration and Requirements states that 13 Republican controlled statehouses around the United States are requiring photo identification at the polls. Moreover, they want to reduce the number of early voting days and tighten registration rules. In May 2011, states like Wisconsin and Texas recently signed bills into laws joining South Carolina and Kansas.

After the 2000 Presidential election between George W. Bush and Al Gore, Republicans have been pushing for some kind of voter registration and requirements. All attempts were derailed when the Bush 43rd Administration fired United States attorneys accusing them of not aggressively pursuing voter fraud. But since the 2010 mid-term elections, Republicans control 59 chambers of the legislatures and 29 governorships. This allowed the bills to move forward and their long-held dream is soon becoming a reality.

Democrats point out that these new provisions will discourage voters from going to the poll to vote. They also say that these laws hearken back to the days of Jim Crow with poll tax and literacy test that was placed on African-Americans mainly in the South from the period of Reconstruction to the 1960's- that lasted over 100 years. Democrats go on to say that these laws are targeted at minorities, poor people, students, and the elderly-people who tend to vote for Democrats.

In Conclusion

Voting is a given right as an American citizen. The United States Constitution protects the voting rights for minorities and women from this kind of injustice. This is why the Civil Rights movement happened- its main effort was to provide minorities with an opportunity to vote. I hope that members of the ACLU and the U.S. Justice Department would sue these 13 States for violating the U.S. Constitution and the Voting Right Act. These laws are clearly illegal and need to be stopped. This is a sad day for the Republican Party if they can't win on ideas- they choose to steal elections instead.

June21st

Stop!! No Saggy Pants Allowed

On Wednesday June 15th, a 20-year-old football player from the University of New Mexico named Deshon Marman was charged for failing to pull his saggy pants on an US Airway Flight 488 out of San Francisco International airport. The following day, the San Francisco police reported that the captain of the flight made a citizen's arrest after Mr. Marman refused to obey his command. When Mr. Marman walked off the airplane he was met by San Francisco police officers and struggled not to be handcuffed according to police reports.

To add injury to insult, Mr. Marman was in town to attend the funeral of his best friend and former teammate David Henderson. The attorney who is representing Mr. Marman is hoping to get the charges dropped. The spokesman for US Airway had no comment on the incident but went on to say that the company doesn't have a detailed dress code for their passengers.

In conclusion

The airline industry does not have a clear dress code for their passenger and without it the airline industry is leaving themselves open to cries of discrimination and lawsuits. The airline industry has enough to worry about than the appearance of someone's wardrobe. If the man paid for his ticket, went through airlines security and they didn't have a problem why should the captain. A word of advice, captain your job is to fly the plane safely. Your job is not to play fashion police. Do your job!!

June 23rd

Shut Up and Vote!!

In the United States, we debate about everything. We even debate about debates. With the advent of talk radio and the internet more people can voice their options freely. However, with all this comes anonymity to say and write what you feel without being responsible for the content.

When the topic of politics is discussed, the critics from the far left and right always say the most ridiculous things - they are instigators. On several occasions, some of these people proudly say they do not vote. What? This is troubling.

Most of these malcontents are angry at the world for something or another. They think that the political system doesn't work for them and that their votes won't count. The far left will bring up the Presidential Election of 2000 and 2004. The far right will bring up the 1992 election. Both are valid points, however, if you don't vote how can you complain about anything?

In the early days of the Republic, only white men who owned land could vote but now that privilege is granted for all American citizens. So when I hear anyone complaining about an issue and proudly proclaim that they do not vote just irritates me to no end. It shows a total disregard for the men and women who were beaten and died for the right for all to vote.

I think about the civil rights movement and how voting was a means to determine their future. I think about the long struggle for woman suffrage and to be on equal footing with their male counterparts. I think about the men and women in the armed services that are fighting and dying for the right for all of us to exercise our right to vote.

People have the right to their options but when a person does not exercise their right to vote it's a slap in the face to all the men and women mentioned before. Talk is cheap and action speaks louder than words. When election time comes around -shut up and vote. Do your civic duty, so when you bitch, you do have something to bitch about.

June 28th

Michael Jackson Remembered

This weekend was the 2nd Anniversary of Michael Jackson's death. The anniversary received little to no fanfare around the world. The man who brought so much joy to millions of people was a little more than a footnote to many news and music organizations. However, the people who loved this man's talent and music remembered.

From the time that he could walk, he entertained and amazed us with his talent as an all-around entertainer. Although in his later life he had trouble with the law and fighting personal demons, he continued to give his all to the fans that marveled at his talent.

Here's to you M.J., we hope you're finally at peace. And despite your trials and tribulations people out there still love you. We (your fans) hope that you found the peace in death that had evaded you throughout your entire life. Rest in Peace.

The Malcontents: Volume 1

Webster's New Collegiate Dictionary defines the word Malcontent as *a discontented person: **a** one who bears a grudge from a sense of thwarted ambition **b**: one who is in active opposition to an established order of government: REBEL.* In the United States there are two groups that are the true sense of this definition- the far left and the neo-conservatives. Both groups seem to be in opposition with reason. Furthermore, when either group gets what they want -they're still not satisfied. Their personal agendas get in the way of the greater good of the people as a whole. First, we will examine the far left and their motives and then in volume 2 –neo conservatives.

Most people in America view the far left as tree hugging, long hair freaks that still live as hippies, eating organic food, and smoking dope all day while listening to Pink Floyd. This imagined image is far from the truth. The far left movement is more complex than that. The far left agenda is to fund their movement even to the peril of the same people who try to champion their causes. The people on the far left are not content with some victories- they either want it all or nothing at all. This is not logical or practical in our American democracy.

For example, let's take the issue of Gays serving openly in the military. When the LGBT community asked the Clinton Administration to take up the issue they didn't think about the political ramification and how this could affect Mr. Clinton's bid for re-election. The political and national heat that the administration received was harsh and brutal- especially from the military. The compromise was the *Don't Ask, Don't Tell* policy. The LGBT community wasn't satisfied and dismissed the Clinton Administration for not doing enough. Now let us fast forward to the Obama Administration for lifting the ban on the *Don't Ask, Don't Tell* policy- now some in the LGBT community are saying that his Administration didn't lift the ban quickly enough-that's gratitude for you. I didn't see them pressing the Bush 43rd Administration on that same issue. This is just one example of hundreds of examples why the far left are professional malcontents.

Real Intentions - A friend who worked for a non-profit told me that the rate of donations are down because President Obama is in office and that they need to fight him on issues even if they agree with him so they can raise funding. What? That doesn't make any sense? So they're fighting the same administration that could possibly advance their cause- that's unbelievable.

Final Analysis - The far left are professional malcontents because it pays to be one. If history is our guide- the agenda process takes time. Americans have to warm up to certain issues- that's the way it has always been for better or worse. Screaming loud and imitating people won't make them embrace your causes- in fact it will have the opposite effect. In my opinion, the far left makes a living off the discontentment found on the fringes of our society. They really don't care if legislation gets passed or not. Just keep the money rolling in.

Camper Trailer. Berkeley, CA

The Malcontents: Volume 2

Webster's New Collegiate Dictionary defines the word Malcontent as *a discontented person: **a** one who bears a grudge from a sense of thwarted ambition **b**: one who is in active opposition to an established order of government: REBEL.* In the United States there are two groups that are the true sense of this definition- the far left and the neo-conservatives. Both groups seem to be in opposition of reason. In Volume 1, we discussed the motives of the far left. Now in Volume 2, we will examine neo-conservatives in the same manner.

Most people in America view the neo conservatives as white, racist, religious freaks who long for the early days of the republic (slavery and laissez- faire laws). This is not altogether true. The neo-conservative movement is more complex than that. Their agenda is to protect the wealthiest among us. They will use patriotism, racism, divisionism and fear as weapons of choice. These people feel privileged and have no qualms to destroy anyone or anything that gets in their way.

For example, take the issue of the debt ceiling. The neo-conservatives in Congress are using this issue as leverage to get the Democrats to protect oil subsidies and cut taxes for corporations and wealthy Americans. They are willing to bring down the excellent credit rating of the U.S. and cause another global recession/depression to get what they want- protection for the wealthy. This is Trickle-Down Economics taken to the extreme. These same tax cuts that neo-conservatives want is the same policies that led us to this global recession in the first place.

Real Intentions -Neo-conservative movements like the Tea Party are all a front for wealthy white men to influence the Republican Party not to abandon the Trickle-Down Economic theory championed by former President Ronald Reagan. Neo- conservative talk shows and neo-conservative cable channels (namely Fox News) are propaganda tools for the wealthy to stroke the white man's political outrage. Then every once in a while they throw in some token minority to confirm their belief of how America should be-white, wealthy and free.

Final Analysis - The neo-conservatives are malcontents because they want to maintain their way of life. If you do not run in the same circles or subscribe to their way of thinking then you are the enemy and un-American. As a whole, they are unwilling to compromise or work with others to find a common sense solution to problems. It's their way or nothing at all. It's funny that Rupert Murdoch, the leader of this neo-conservative movement is an Australian. How American is that? This movement is a farce- it's time to put it out of its misery.

Students Protest against College Republicans mock Affirmative Action Bake Sale – 2011, UC Berkeley, California

Check Out My Index Finger!!!

If you want to figure out the penis size of a man you do not have to wait any longer. Forget about looking at a man's feet or hands- it's his index finger that will give the true measure.

Dr. Tae Beom Kim, an urologist at Gachon University in Incheon, Korea, and his colleagues studied 144 men over the age of 20 who were undergoing urological surgery. One of the researchers measured the patient's penile length — flaccid and stretched — just after they went under anesthesia for their operations, and another researcher measured their finger length. After the data was collected and stored Dr. Kim wrote the following about the research:

Previous studies have linked the so-called 2D:4D ratio of finger length with exposure to the sex hormones estrogen and testosterone in the womb. So it's plausible that the same exposure may affect penis length.

In other words, if a man's index finger is shorter than his ring finger than the man has a rather large penis.

This digit ratio research has been done before. Most recently in 2000, researchers at UC Berkeley reported that lesbians have a two finger length that was typical of men. Needless to say, that this conclusion was controversial at the time.

July 19th

Carpe Diem

For those who read the *1lovejoy* blog, you are well aware of this blog's disdain for Rupert Murdoch's questionable journalistic practices, his business dealings and neo conservative politics. It's not surprising that Mr. Murdoch's companies are in a bit of a pickle. He has weathered scandal before but somehow this phone-hacking scandal is different. It shows how Mr. Murdoch and his hand-picked lieutenants created a culture of pay-offs and intimidation. It seemed to be inevitable that one of his news media outlets would take things too far in order to get a story.

In a recent New *York Times* article, reporter David Carr wrote about pay-offs and phone- hacking in the United States (2006 Minnesota and 2009 New Jersey). All of these events were chronicled before the British newspaper *The Guardian* exposed the scandal in Britain.

Law makers from Britain and America need to send a clear message to Mr. Murdoch- NO MORE!! No more to tolerating tabloid and hearsay journalism. No more intimidating politicians for political favors or because they may disagree on a particular issue or ideology that Mr. Murdoch subscribes to. No more to his neo-McCarthyism brand of justice.

If the United States and Great Britain believe in a free press- I pray that news media outlets and politicos investigate News Corp and News International's under-handed dealings on both sides of the pond. Just like India and China, I hope that the U.S. and Britain will reject the Murdoch brand and marginalize him to obscurity.

However, as stated in the beginning of this article, Mr. Murdoch thinks he can weather this storm if he says "I'm Sorry" and throws a few bucks at the problem. With this breach of trust - his integrity has gone out the window. His creditability will forever be questioned.

Mark Lewis, the lawyer for the Family of the murdered British girl, Milly Dowler, said it best about the culture of News Corp and News International - "This is not just about one individual but about the culture of an organization."

July 21ˢᵗ

The Empire Strikes Back

In the United States there is a sickness that's going around. The symptom that is diagnosed is that rich or affluent people in the United States are money hungry and want to maintain power by any means necessary. We will examine this disease by looking at some case studies. The results of this study may not shock you but reaffirm what you already know-especially in this so called worldwide recession that they created.

Sports

The National Football League (NFL) and the National Basketball Association (NBA) called for Lockouts in their respective leagues. Both leagues claim that they are losing money and they want to renegotiate the terms of their contracts with their players unions for a new deal. In other words, they want more money and more control over players movements (especially of their star players).

The Players Union from each side wanted the owners to open their accounting books to check if the owners were really losing money. In the NFL, only one team showed their books to the unions and the others teams flat-out refused. In the NBA, the owners of 22 teams said that they are losing money. However, the union found that only 9 teams had a legitimate claim.

Politics

The Republican Party (especially the fringe group calling themselves the Tea Party) are holding up the passage of the debt ceiling to demand more tax breaks for the wealthy and corporations. The debt ceiling has always been a non-issue that passed with ease for every President who held the office. Never before has this been a major issue because the United States always pays its bills.

America's wealthiest people are enjoying record low taxes and they aim to keep it that way even if the least of their brethren has to suffer. This is a stance for supply side economics (trickle-down economics) and people who champion that belief.

Business

The business communities are upset about government wanting to enact regulations on businesses. They feel that with government oversight the free market will suffer and that it will limit their ability to compete.

With a lack of government oversight the free market took a terrible dive. Wall Street actions brought us all to the brink of a worldwide depression. Today, businesses are making record profits because of tax payer's bailout money but businesses are not hiring people and are cutting staff to make more of a profit. In some cases one person is doing the job that is intended for multiple people. That's efficiency (according to the powers that be).

In Conclusion

The three examples that were given are symptoms of rich, angry people. The problem is greed; the cure- there is no cure for people who feel entitled. All of their lives they have been afforded opportunities that few of us have and for reassurance they hang around people of their same ilk. All of these issues are about asserting power. In their mind, they feel that they're losing their hold of that power. If you're the person hiring and firing, if you're the person who controls the financial systems, if you're the person who has all the advantages to do what you want- how do you feel that you are losing your grip on power? This is the sickness-there is no immediate cure.

Artwork displaying dissenting voice of NFL fans. Finn McCool's, New Orleans, LA.

An Artist Remembered: Amy Winehouse

This blog is remembering the life and death of Amy Winehouse. This 27 year old neo-soul singer's personal struggle with drug and alcohol addiction was difficult to watch. For those who followed her, many hoped she'd kick her habit. Alas, it was never to be. Another talented person gone too soon.

Notable Songs:

What Is It About Men (from the album *Frank*)

Stronger Than Me (from the album *Frank*)

Back To Black (from the album *Back To Black*)

Rehab (from the album *Back To Black*)

Tears Dry On Their Own (from the album *Back To Black*)

August 2nd

Happy Birthday, Mr. President

In the beginning of 2009, President George W. Bush and his administration left the American people and the rest of the world with 8 years of shitty government. His administration managed to involve the United States (and the world) in 2 wars, a record trade deficit, a record national debt, a global recession, a world gripped in fear and the U.S. international reputation in shambles. Those horrific years seemed a distant memory thanks to a man who had hope for his country and the world - President Obama.

In a little less than 2 years, President Obama restored the United States to good international standing; caught Osama Bin Laden, averted another

"Great Depression"; started the effort to end the wars in the Middle East; held an oil company (BP) responsible for the gulf coast oil spill and cleanup efforts; reformed health care and the financial industries; reformed FEMA; saved the U.S. auto industry; reduced nuclear arms with Russia; repealed the don't ask don't tell military policy; signed the equal pay for equal work for women act; signed an executive order to shut down the infamous prison "Gitmo"; promoted green technology to end dependence on fossil fuel and extended military veterans benefits . Yet, he is faced with obstructionist from the opposition and his own party every step of the way.

Being the President of the United States is a hardest job in the world and it must take a further toll when your birthright, integrity, religious beliefs and manhood is questioned, plus the added pressure of being the first African-American to hold office. It would drive a normal person to scream at the top of their lungs but he seems to take it all in stride. Like a good chess player he anticipates every move that will come from his so-called friends and foes alike. He is truly graceful under pressure.

Mr. President, for those who admire what you are doing, we salute you. We salute you because the job you took on was not an easy one. You tried to change politics as usual but the powers that be are hell-bent to keep things the way they are. You're just one man with one voice telling the people that you need their help to bring about change. We the American people have let you down. We were easily distracted by a "Tea Party", "The Decision", and celebrities behaving badly. We thought the night you were elected that everything would change in a heartbeat after the Bush Era. We now know that change takes time.

I like to take this time to apologize for the American people –in fact the world- for not heeding your call for help. You said," *Power will not concede without a fight*", and judging by current world events that's what is happening. The one President that faced the same issues that you are encountering would be President Franklin D. Roosevelt. The similarities are profound. If history is to be our guide, like FDR, you will find a way to truly change America and the world and become one of the greatest Presidents known to date.

Mr. President, believe in us because the majority of the American public (and the world) believes in you. You have a shitty job and everyone knows it. As the British playwright William Shakespeare wrote, *"Do not be afraid of greatness...Some men are born great...some men achieve greatness...And some men have greatness trust upon them."* We all see the greatness in you. Just believe in us–even though we may let you down from time to time.

Then Senator Barack Obama at Tulane University on Campaign Swing. 2008 New Orleans, LA.

What Happened to Sean Hoare?

On July 18th, the former veteran show business correspondent for the newspaper *News of the World*, died in his home located in Watford (a suburb of London). Police said his death was "unexplained" and "not thought to be suspicious". It was noted that Mr. Hoare had a history of drug and alcohol abuse but the toxicology test is still pending.

The reason why Mr. Hoare's death is so unique is because he was the whistle-blower that exposed the phone-hacking scandal involving The Murdoch Empire along with the rest of their loyal lieutenants. He told the *New York Times* as early as September 2010 that Andy Coulson (Prime Minister Cameron former Communication Director) was aware of phone-hacking practices at *News of the World* and *The Sun*. The Milly Dowler case exposed and weakened the Murdoch brand and the power wheeled by one mogul.

It was a bit ironic that Mr. Hoare died the day before Mr. Rupert & James Murdoch testified before a committee of Parliament. Moreover, friends and colleagues reported that Mr. Hoare had cleaned up his act (not abusing drugs & alcohol).

The one man that knew all the parties involved is suddenly dead. A healthy man in his mid- 40's just expired? I'm no conspiracy theorist but its strange timing. The autopsy of Amy Winehouse was done in 2 days and but there is still no report explaining Mr. Hoare's death.

Mr. Hoare said often that he hoped that the phone-hacking scandal would lead to journalism "Being cleaned up." I truly hope that responsible journalism comes back in vogue and that his death stood for the end of yellow journalism.

August 9th

Blame Yourself America!!

In the midterm election of 2010, the American public decided to elect Republicans to Congress thereby sending a message to President Obama that they were going to slow down his agenda. Most of these members consider themselves to be Tea Party members and have little to no experience in politics. They ran on the agenda of 'No New Taxes'; repealed the new healthcare law and displayed their bitter disdain for the President (basically because he's African–American). These people were hell bent to obstruct the Obama Administration. With this agenda they managed to bring down an entire nation with them.

Just recently, Standard & Poor's (S&P) downgraded America's credit rating from AAA to AA+. The main factor that was given for the downgrade was because of the "*degree of uncertainty around the political policy process...the nature of the debate and the difficulty in framing a political consensus*" In other words, because of the Tea Party's inability to compromise - the U.S. will face this impasse in the future.

Congratulations America!! You voted these nut jobs into office and if you didn't vote at all-you might has well just have voted for them. Why did you do this to our country? Was it because of your racist hatred for the President or was it apathy that did it to you. No matter the reason, you guys fucked up!! Now interest rates will go up. In laymen's terms, prices will go up on everything- food, gas, mortgage rates on credit cards, home mortgage, car loans, and student loans- Catch my drift. It will be like we are living overseas where everything is small and expensive (no value for your buck). You really did it this time.

How Did We Get Here?

The Tea Party was the creation of the Murdoch machine and conservative talk radio host. They created tension with the Obama Administration from day 1 to undermine the massive cleanup job that awaited him after the Bush 43rd presidency. They wanted to keep their way of life intact.

I believe that the Tea Party has won the battle but lost the war. The American public finally saw these people for whom they truly are- racist, bigots, uncompromising, and uneducated fools. Their agenda is clear- protect the wealthy and corporations at all cost.

What Must We Do?

America you have enough time to change this course. In the 2012 elections you have the power to vote these nut jobs out of office. From time to time you are allowed to make a mistake. Now since you learnt from your mistake- let's right the ship. We have been living off the fat of the land for about 10 years-now it's time to pay the piper. Everyone has to sacrifice- that means cuts to entitlement programs and taxing the rich. This is a balanced approach that the President has called for.

Let's face it, we have to make sacrifices to maintain the lifestyle we want to live. Let's elect people in office that are able to work together. This has always been the American way. This experiment of political bullying should quickly come to an end - so ends the lesson.

August 18th

Armageddon...Take 2

As we draw closer to the end of August and look forward to September we all know that doom is coming. I don't mean the Tea Party, but a more menacing force that will quickly come upon the horizon. Once again doom and terror will grip the world on October 21st. It's Armageddon time.

On October 21st, Mr. Harold Camping and his organization Family Radio is warning the world of doom and gloom once again. After his missed prediction of the world's doom on March 21st- reports said he was stunned and flabbergasted. To Mr. Camping's credit, he admitted that his calculations were wrong and that October 21st was sure to be the date that the world would end.

On the Family Radio website, an explanation was given for the miscalculation of his prediction. This is just a sampling of the argument given:

Thus we can be sure that the whole world, with the exception of those who are presently saved (the elect), are under the judgment of God, and will be annihilated together with the whole physical world on October 21, 2011, on the last day of the present five months period. On that day the true believers (the elect) will be raptured. We must remember that only God knows who His elect are that He saved prior to May 21.

It seemed like Mr. Camping didn't learn his lesson or his math once again. This blog stated before that Mr. Camping is an 89 year old man with nothing to lose and wants to be remembered for something. After his massive stroke the only one who is going meet his maker on October 21st might be Mr. Camping.

August 25th

Remembering Hurricane Katrina

On the morning of August 29, 2005, a category three hurricane stuck the Gulf Coast of the United States. The aftermath of the disaster was the most costly in U.S. history. An estimated $81 Billion dollars in damages occurred and left one of the oldest and most beloved American cities in near ruins.

Lost Trust

Hurricane Katrina wasn't just a natural disaster but a wake-up call for America and the world. It exposed the Bush 43rd Administration as incompetent in dealing with domestic affairs; it exposed slow bureaucratic government red tape; it exposed corruption in a major American city; it exposed a power struggle between all levels of government but it also exposed the poverty and wealth gap that exists in America. In other words-America was exposed.

This event was the downfall of the Bush presidency as the lack of leadership from him or his cabinet was apparent. It was amazing that he could send American citizens to fight for other people's freedom around the world but his administration failed to protect and serve his fellow Americans. At that point, his administration lost all credibility.

The Comeback

The city of New Orleans with the rest of the Gulf Coast that was affected by the hurricane is making a comeback. Slowly but surely people are taking their future in their own hands and not depending on the government to help them out. People share a laugh or two about government red tape in the thick humid air over libations talking about what they've lost and what they've gained.

This is the spirit of New Orleans and the Gulf Coast- have a laugh and take whatever comes. This is a lesson for the rest of America and the world, you can make a comeback. If you have the will and the desire to fight- then you can make it.

Overcoming

With the start of the NFL season, the city of New Orleans will be rooting for Drew Brees and the New Orleans Saints to bring back another Super Bowl Championship and gearing up for the upcoming carnival season. But, never far from the thoughts of every New Orleanian (near or aboard) is that terrible day when Hurricane Katrina came ashore. We hope we taught America a lesson about the poor in this country, we hope we taught the lesson about community and how people should help one another. We hope that we taught the world about our resilient spirit. As we remember the lessons taught by Hurricane Katrina, let us remember that the will to live and fight on is an enduring spirit in the human race. Let's Geaux SAINTS!!!

Pat O'Brien's. New Orleans, LA.

Muammar Hearts Leezza

When the Rebel fighters in Libya captured the Gaddafi compound, they never dreamed of finding Muammar Gaddafi's little scrapbook. The contents of the scrapbook had pictures of Mr. Gaddafi's one true love- former Secretary of State- Condoleezza Rice.

I was thinking if Mr. Gaddafi had written a love letter to the former Secretary of State- it would go a little something like this:

> *Dear Leezza,*
>
> *My strong black African princess, I was just dreaming of you. I wish that you can come over to my tent so we can spend a little time with each other. I know W. is working you like a dog trying to cover up all his mistakes. But with me all you have to do is relax and be yourself.*
>
> *I was thinking the other day of the first time I met you. The way you smiled at me and shook my hand, I thought I was going to melt with delight. And the way you ordered the Arabs leaders around just turned me on. Right then and there- I knew you were the one for me.*
>
> *I know you're busy with your job at the moment, but when you are completely done saving W's ass, come to me as soon as you can. I swear to you, you don't have to worry about a thing- I have billions in the bank.*
>
> *Just remember, you will forever be the lady in my life.*
>
> *Forever Yours,*
>
> *Muammar*
>
> **Dictator of Libya**

Can Ecstasy Cure Cancer?

In 2006, a research team at the University of Birmingham (U.K.) led by lead researcher Professor John Gordon showed that modified ecstasy and anti-depressants (i.e. Prozac) could potentially stop some blood cancers from growing.

The researchers at the University of Birmingham along with researchers at the University of Western Australia, have chemically altered ecstasy by taking away some atoms and replacing it with new ones. Professor John Gordon told the BBC the following about the research:

> *Against the cancers, particularly the leukemia, the lymphoma and the myeloma, where we've tested these new compounds we can wipe out 100% of the cancer cells in some cases.*

In the scientific community there is genuine excitement about this breakthrough in cancer research. If all goes well, a drug, will still be at least 10 years away.

September 6th

9/11: A Retrospective

In a little less than 10 years, President Obama announced that Osama Bin Laden was dead. His death closed the chapter on a horrific day in human history. This week will mark the tenth anniversary when terror from aboard reached America's shore. This event, so surreal in its scope seemed just like a movie.

It was hard not to think about the people that you loved on that day. You found yourself reaching out to family, friends, and close neighbors that you haven't contacted in years just to check if they were okay. On that day, we forgot about ourselves and thought about other people. In a sense, we were all a little more humane that day. Fast forward to the present and it seems like we have forgotten the lessons we learned that day. We replaced it with fear, doubt, and cynicism, we reversed back to the people we were before 9/11.

When we started suspecting people of a non-Judeo-Christian faith we lost our innocence and humanity. Some became blood-thirsty and vengeful and allowed certain liberties to be obstructed in the name of safety and security. We lost our way.

Let's get back to that feeling after 9/11 when we hug each other just a little longer, talk to each other a little longer and say *I love you* to someone we really care about . Let get back to that feeling when we all cared for one another-can we?

September 22nd

To Serve with Pride

On Tuesday, the long standing military policy of *don't ask, don't tell* was repealed. For conservatives this action is a blow to their steadfast belief that the military should be 100% heterosexual. And to the LGBT community this policy change means that one can serve openly in the military without fear of reprisals.

Fear

From personal experience, as a veteran of the military, there are Gays and Lesbians in the military and everyone who works with these individuals knows who they are. They only tell close colleagues or people who will not judge them. They always lived with the constant threat that they would be found out and lose their career and benefits they worked so hard to achieve.

History

Sexual orientation has no relationship with leadership skills and we have examples in History to support this claim. Two of the greatest military leaders, Alexander the Great and Julius Caesar were bisexual and were able to lead military campaigns with outstanding results. J. Edgar Hoover was the longest servicing FBI Director and he was gay and very conservative.

I hope that repealing this law will forever end the discussion that the LGBT community can't serve their country because of their sexual orientation. The conservatives are just delusional in their way of thinking on this matter. If the military is fine with it- then America should be fine with it as well.

September 27th

Japan: Six Months Later

Japan has become transformed after the events of the deadly tsunami and radiation disaster that followed. It seemed that the country was heading for the worst human horror ever foreseen and it appeared that all was lost in the land of the rising sun- or was it.

The resilient people of Japan refused to go down without a fight and went to work trying to rebuild what was lost. First, the people wanted answers from their government-as a result- a new Prime Minister was elected. Secondly, they wanted answers from the people who ran the ill-fated Fukushima Daiichi nuclear plant. As a result, their government is keeping the company's feet to the fire to clean up the nuclear waste and holding them accountable.

With the recent typhoon, misinformation from the government, corrupt nuclear plant operators and a stream of disappointing news one would think that the Japanese people would cry to the sky and say- *Why Us*? However, the Japanese people go on living their lives. They hope for the best and brace themselves for the worst. They just keep pressing on.

With the entire world in fiscal and political upheaval, we should look to the Japanese people and their resolve throughout their many trials and tribulations. For in the people of Japan, we see grace under pressure and an enduring spirit that will never quit. Japan, keep pressing on- the world is behind you.

October 6th

99 Percent

There is a movement in the United States that is slowly taking shape. This movement is made up of people of every gender, color and creed. This movement generally comprises young people of a working age that are unemployed. They believed that if they follow the rules deemed by society that they would be rewarded-but in this era of selfishness- this is not the case. So this group, the 99 percent, are occupying Wall Street to show the powers that be what their selfishness and greed is doing to general public.

Mass Media

The mass media is giving this movement very little coverage. They rather focus on old, crusty, bigots who do not want to do their fair share in the society that they live (the Tea Party). The media at large thinks because a person is older that they are more likely to vote than younger people. How soon we forget the lesson of 2008 when an unknown Senator from Illinois became President of the United States because of the power of youth vote.

Their Mission Statement

The 99 percent mission statement is clear and straight to the point:

Occupy Wall Street is a leaderless resistance movement with people of many colors, genders and political persuasions. The one thing we all have in common is that We Are The 99% that will no longer tolerate the greed and corruption of the 1%. We are using the revolutionary Arab Spring tactic to achieve our ends and encourage the use of nonviolence to maximize the safety of all participants.

Reinforcements

It seems that the Labor Union movement in the United States is seeing an opportunity to aid the *Occupy Wall Street* movement. The unions will send supplies, people and money to aid in the fight for Wall Street to redistribute jobs and wealth in this economy.

Last Words

The 99 percent are practicing civil disobedience in the true sense of the word-unlike their Tea Party counterparts. Wall Street and the banks are making record profits because they were aided by a tax payer bailout. The people in the United States though that if we take care of them then they will surely take care of us. Instead the tax payers got screwed by the powers that be. This group – the 99 percent- had enough of bickering politicians; had enough of Tea Party politics; had enough of Wall Street getting away with everything under the sun. The mission statement said it best about this movement, "We Are The 99% *that will no longer tolerate the greed and corruption of the 1%"*. Let it be known that the common person is frustrated with Wall Street, Tea Party politics and their tomfoolery- you were warned!

October 11th

What Were Steve Jobs' Last Words?

On October 5th- the co-founder of Apple –Steve Jobs- expired from the earth. Many tributes and make shift memorials were dedicated in his honor. The legacy of Steve Jobs touches us all in some small way; whether we are aware of it or not. In the many dedications that were bestowed on Mr. Jobs in the last week- no one thought to ask, *what were his last words?*

Theory

When a person dies- a word or words are spoken. The last word (or words) is important because it delves deep into the soul of a person. It clarifies and cuts through the barriers and walls that one puts up in their life to protect them from the cruel world. The last word that is uttered from someone's lips is just as important as the first word uttered out from the mouth of a babe. The last words mean something much more than one realizes.

Reality

Many friends and colleagues said that Mr. Jobs valued his privacy. If Mr. Jobs had any last words to say it would be to his wife and kids. His last words were meant for them. We can speculate until the cows come home but we will never really know until we are meant to know.

Conclusion

Steve Jobs completed a biography about his life with former TIME magazine managing editor Walter Isaacson (that will be published on October 24th by Simon & Schuster). And of course Sony Picture secured the rights to the unpublished biography to make into a movie. Nevertheless, when asked why he was writing his biography- Mr. Jobs replied, "*I wanted my kids to know me.*" Maybe in that eloquent statement that's all that he wanted- for his kids to see him as a person and not the icon. Maybe that is his last words to the world- see him as a real person. That's not difficult to understand at all- or is it?

Occupy

On October 15, there were Occupy protest rallies all across America and the World and I decided to check out firsthand what the mood was like by going to one of these rallies. The atmosphere was peaceful; the people in the crowd were from every shade and socioeconomic background. Unlike the Klu Klux Klan- like rallies held by the Tea Party- the Occupy movement felt like a cry for reasonable people to come together and fix what is ailing the worldwide economy.

Demands

Most Politicians and the main stream media want to know what the Occupy Movement demands are and how fast can they fix them. If the politicians and the main stream media listen carefully they know what the problem is-apathy, selfishness, and greed.

The Frontline

I interviewed 3 Registered Nurses who came to the march to make their voices heard. As I talked to them they told me stories about having to kick people out of the hospital beds because they couldn't pay their medical bills and how the Insurance companies were raising premiums and medication that patients can't afford.

Power Struggle

We are in a power struggle for change. In one corner- the old guard (Tea Party) like things the way they are. And in the other corner are the children of the old guard (99 percent) saying that things have to change or we all fail. President Obama said it best, *"Power will not concede without a fight"* and by the looks of things he is absolutely correct.

Who Is To Blame

We are all to blame for this situation. We thought that by electing President Obama that he will change everything overnight. He asked for our help to push the change agenda and instead we voted in an obstructionist Republican Congress because they used your fear against you. Now you're upset because you realize that government needs to be run by reasonable people. Rome was not built in a day and it took the United States 10 years of mismanagement to get us in this situation. This is not a fast food solution- this will take time.

Personal Note

On a personal note, I was encouraged to see that people have had enough of Wall Street not contributing to the economic recovery effort. They got theirs through a tax payer bailout, but don't know how to give us ours. As I always stress in this blog- education and compromise is how reasonable solutions comes about. The demands from the protestors should be self-explanatory- put in what you take out- pay it forward. As an American I was glad to see people coming together to voice their opinion in this critical matter. Hopefully, the actions of the Occupy movement will turn into votes for people who want to work for solutions and not people who play games to gain power.

People take to the streets, Occupy Wall Street protest. 2011 San Francisco, CA

People take to the streets, Occupy Wall Street protest. 2011 San Francisco, CA

People take to the streets, Occupy Wall Street protest. 2011 San Francisco, CA

October 25th

Vindication

Last week President Obama received news that the Libyan dictator Colonial Gaddafi was captured and killed. Later on, during the week- the President announced that all remaining U.S. troops from Iraq will be home for the upcoming holidays. These two events vindicated President Obama's foreign strategy and also kept the promise he made as a candidate running for the presidency.

Iraq-Reality

The hawks in Congress and the Republican Presidential Candidates would like the President to keep troops in Iraq to stabilize the situation before leaving. The reality is that Iraq is as stable as its going to be, so staying there ten more years is not going to make a big difference. We have wasted too much time, money, manpower and resources behind a war that was a revenge mission for Bush 43 against Saddam Hussein who attempted to assassinate his father –Bush 41.

Moreover, President Obama is honoring the agreement that the Bush 43rd administration made with the Iraqi government. Iraq could not and would not protect our troops from prosecution by the Iraqi legal system- the choice was clear- they wanted the U.S gone. The action by the Iraqi's made the decision easy for the President to bring our troops home.

Libya-Reality

The decision to help the Libyan people was made because Gaddafi and his regime threatened to commit genocide on their own people. The President wanted to prevent this genocide even though the Right and the Left criticized his action and said that he was involving the U.S. in another war. A member of his own party even threatened an impeachment hearing on the President's decision. To his credit- he stood by his principles and succeeded (along with the help of NATO) to aid the Libyan rebels in the capture and killing of Gaddafi and his regime.

Election Cycle Politics

Since we are in an election cycle, his friends and foes alike are not giving the President his due. The same people that were quick to criticize are giving credit to others and patting themselves on the back. The President is not the type of man to brag about his accomplishment but he should be happy with what he achieved under dire circumstances. It's amazing what the President can do without an obstructionist Congress getting in the way.

Conclusion

President Obama should receive all the credit for his achievement is his endeavors to clear up the image of the U.S. aboard. The cookie cutter strategy that the Bush 43rd administration implemented did not work- it failed horribly. President Obama is showing that intelligence gathering, strategic targeting and diplomacy is the way to understand the true nature and intent of your friends and enemies alike. This is the way foreign policy should be done- this is the new template- the new way forward.

October 27th

Scary Things

In keeping with the spirit of the Halloween season-I would like to share my deepest fears with the 1Lovejoy nation. These are just a few thoughts that frighten and keep me up in the middle of the night. Without further ado here are a few scary scenarios.

A conservative and non-compassionate U.S. Supreme Court
Corporations and Big Banks not being punished for the "Great Recession"
Another tsunami striking Japan
Another breach in the levee system that protects New Orleans
Gaddafi's son(s) coming back to Libya to start a civil war
The build—up of the Chinese Naval Fleet
The Pakistani government knowingly harboring terrorist(s)
Iran actually having nuclear weapons
A Republican actually becoming President in 2012
The Mayans 2012 End of the World prediction
The Tea Party Republicans still retaining control of Congress in 2012
Harold Camping making another End of the World prediction
Rupert Murdoch and his lieutenants not being punished for the phone-hacking scandal
Republican's stealing the 2012 election
People's apathy
Racial and gender inequality
Religious and political extremists
Mormons
Fox News
Conservative Talk Radio
The Greece economic crisis
The collapse of the Euro Zone
The merchandising of the Occupy Movement
Richard Nixon, Ronald Reagan or George W. Bush becoming President again.

These are just a few things to ponder. Have a Happy and safe Halloween weekend.

What Were Steve Jobs Last Words? : Volume 2

If you've haven't heard by now- Steve Jobs last words were revealed this week by his sister Mona Simpson. During her eulogy about her beloved brother- she mentioned his last words were, *"Oh Wow. Oh Wow. Oh Wow."*

These words were uttered when Mr. Jobs was in and out of consciousness during his last hours on earth. However, his last words revealed something deeper- a whole lot deeper.

Theory

The movie All That Jazz is the 1979 Academy Award winning musical about a director/ choreographer Bob Fosse and his life in the entertainment business. Mr. Fosse's alter ego in the movie (and main character) is named Joe Gideon. Mr. Gideon is a workaholic, who feels like he has to work twice as hard to be perfect his craft.

All of a sudden he has a stroke and the movie quickly centers on his mortality and the book *"On Death and Dying"* by Dr. Elizabeth Kubler-Ross. The movie then discusses the 5 themes in the book about the death process which are: Anger, Denial, Bargaining, Depression, and Acceptance.

Also, note that the main character's catch phrase was *"Oh Wow."*

Conclusion

Did Mr. Jobs see the movie *All That Jazz*? Are there parallels between Gideon and Jobs? Who's to say, but I find the similarities quite remarkable; a man who was a success to everyone but himself; a man that pushed himself until his death; a man that could have gone through the five phases in the death process; a man who uttered the words" Oh Wow." Is this art imitating life? One may never know- but it does make one wonder.

November 8th

In Memory of Andy Rooney

On November 5th, the essayist and commentator, Andy Rooney, passed away at the age of 92. Every Sunday he came into American homes via television to give some good ole' common sense advice to what seemed to be a world out of control. He represented the grandfather that told you the truth when you needed to hear it. He represented that consumer that had enough of false marketing. He represented people who just didn't understand how people can be so cruel to one another. For the people who followed that old grumpy man for many years (including myself) – we will truly miss his candor and his brand of common sense.

November 15th

WATCH OUT!!! You Almost Stepped In That.

There is an illness that has taken the world by storm. In communities everywhere you are bound to see it. This epidemic is people not picking up their dog's shit. That's right I said it.

When people walk their dogs, I wonder if there is a plastic bag on their person so they can retrieve the dog shit that is sure to follow. Nine times out of ten I see no plastic bag with the owner- all I see is an owner being dragged around by their dogs.

To all dog owners (and you know who you are) pick up your dog's shit. If you don't pick up your dog shit it just shows how petty and disgusting you really are. Did you think that dogs didn't shit when you decided to purchase this animal? Did you forget that this animal might want to eat and drink to survive? Did you not realize that this animal has a digestive system? No, I guess you haven't thought about that at all.

So dog lovers-next time you decide to take your dog for a walk- remember to bring a bag with you so if your dog shits you can pick it up. Do the right thing and don't be selfish!

November 17th

The Empire Strikes Back: Volume 2

The powers that be finally struck back. They needed a reason and unfortunately some of the Occupy protesters gave it to them- the health and safety issue.

With all the best intentions of the Occupy Movement- there were some legitimate concerns about debris and pockets of occasional violence in the camps. Businesses that surrounded several of these camps complained to their respective city leaders that the movement was bad for business- in others words- the occupiers had to go.

Politicians, frightened of the business community caved in to their demands and used the shield of health and public safety issue as a cover to protect themselves. Once again, votes and money wins.

What Comes Next

To take a page from the Tea Party- the next phase of the Occupy Movement should be the voting ballot. You have to put pressure on politicians to really reform Wall Street. You have to have a focused message otherwise big business and politicians won't take this movement seriously. Follow the example of Kristen Christian – the woman who organized Bank Transfer Day and got the mighty Bank of America to reverse their policy on debit card charges. The banks had money but she had an idea and people power.

The reason the powers that be think that they can push the movement around is because they think that the people involved have no money and won't vote. If the movement wants to send them a clear message- support the politicians who support your cause. President Obama tried to reform

Wall Street but was met with resistance and obstruction from members of Congress (Tea Party) and conservative state houses. If the movement wants reforms- vote for the people who will get the job done and cater to your terms. Apparently, it worked for the Tea Party and now they control Congress (for the time being).

Get organized, get a focused message and vote for reasonable people. That is how you fight back- that is how the movement will bring down the Death Star. So ends the lesson.

Giving Thanks

In the United States- Thanksgiving is the official start of the holiday season. It's also a time for families to come together and get reacquainted with one another. On this holiday we are to reflect on the many blessings that were bestowed on us this year. A more cynical person would say that this year sucked but I chose to take a different take on this year. To the 1Lovejoy Nation, here's a list for what I'm thankful for this year.

I'm thankful that Osama Bin Laden is dead
I'm thankful that Al-Qaeda is almost destroyed
I'm thankful that George W. Bush is not President
I'm thankful that the Tea Party showed their true colors
I'm thankful that the Occupy Movement woke people up
I'm thankful for the Arab Spring
I'm thankful that Keith Olbermann is sticking it to Fox News and the Conservatives every evening
I'm thankful that this year was better than 2010
I'm thankful to Kristen Christian for organizing Bank Transfer Day
I'm thankful for Japan and the city of New Orleans
I'm thankful that the war in Iraq and Afghanistan will soon come to an end
I'm thankful for the phone-hacking scandal and how it exposed the culture of News Corp/News International
I'm thankful that Harold Camping's End of the World prediction didn't come true
I'm thankful to live in the greatest country in the world
I'm thankful for shelter, food in my stomach and a bed to rest my head
I'm thankful for libations
I'm thankful for the people I met
I'm thankful for the advice I was given
I'm thankful for the wisdom I've gained
I'm thankful to every one of you who follow and read my blog
But most of all- I'm thankful to God for sending me my wife and my family

Take this time to reflect and appreciate all the blessings that is bestowed on you- whether you know it or not. Happy Thanksgiving!!

December 7th

Stocking Stuffer!

If you're running out of ideas this holiday season- there is a product that is sure to peak your interest. The company OhMiBod made the ultimate accessory to the iPod or other MP3 players. This company has created a plug in vibrator so the user can feel the music –literally. On the company's website- it states that, *"it automatically vibrates to the rhythm and intensity of the music."* The website also states that you can join an anonymous club (CLUB VIBE) and share tips on how to get the most of your ohmibod experience. I guess this device gives a whole new meaning to the song *Jingle Bell Rock*. Folks- you can't make this stuff up.

December 14th

Occupy Equals Financiers

The ongoing Occupy San Francisco movement has moved into the second phase- that of financiers. They have plans to create a credit union in the city of San Francisco. On their Facebook page- it states that they want to *"encourage San Francisco residents, businesses, as well as non-profit and city agencies, to keep their money out of the big banks"*. The statement continues by saying that they want to *"redistribute the money locally"* so money can stay in the community.

To show how serious their intentions are, they've registered for the name of their pending credit union with the state of California. They are actively pursuing potential investors in hope to create an *"ideal socially conscious credit union"* as stated on their Facebook page. The initial charter meeting has already taken place.

This is a true turning point for the movement- to see if they're going to help people in need or make profits for their own self-interest. This leaderless, faceless movement has given notice to the powers that be- they're taking over. This movement with young, tech savvy, educated people at the forefront is demanding to be taken seriously. We will wait with abated breath to see if they can succeed in their efforts. Good Luck!!

December 20th

An Offer for Robert Reich

Recently, former Secretary of Labor made some valid observations on President Obama's speech in Kansas about economic equality. He said that he was encouraged and is willing to help the President bring a mandate in his second term. Mr. Reich, on his blog elaborates the key points which will help bring about economic equality:

- Tax Financial transactions
- Use tax revenue to create good schools and access to higher education
- Resurrect the Glass-Steagall Act
- Cap the size of Wall Street
- Require big banks that got bailed out to modify mortgages of Americans that owe more than their homes are worth.

These points are very insightful but overlook some facts. President Obama has tried to implement these ideas but has been obstructed by Congress- on both sides of the aisles. Furthermore, I blame Mr. Reich and the Clinton Administration for putting the U.S. economy in this position.

NAFTA

In December 1993, President Clinton signed the North American Free Trade Agreement (NAFTA). This agreement dates back to the 1986 Reagan-Bush Administration. When George H.W. Bush became President his administration ironed out the details of the deal and signed NAFTA on December 17, 1992. However, the agreement needed to be ratified by each nation's legislative or parliamentary branch and the Clinton Administration brought it home. Mr. Reich was a part of this blitz on Congress to get the deal done. The former Secretary appeared on every media outlet and venue stating that the NAFTA agreement would keep America strong; more than 200,000 jobs would be created and this deal was the best thing for the United States in the long term. Fast forward to the present day and we can see how this deal has worked out; Canada and Mexico have prospered from this deal and America has all but destroyed any hopes of becoming a manufacturing power again.

At the time, Mr. Reich was the mastermind behind the whole strategy to push this deal down the throat of Congress and the American people. In the famous debate between former Vice President Al Gore and Ross Perrot- Mr. Perrot said that "A Giant Sucking Sound" would eliminate millions of jobs in America and move those same jobs overseas. Mr. Perrot lost the debate with Mr. Gore but he had the foresight to see that it was a bad deal and Mr. Reich helped aide and abate this crime.

Gramm-Leach-Bailey Act

In 1999, President Clinton signed the Financial Service Modernization Act (better known as the Gramm-Leach-Bailey Act). This Act repealed parts of the Glass-Steagall Act of 1933 by removing barriers in the market for Banking, securities and insurance companies that profited   from acting as any combination of an investment or commercial bank and an insurance company. In other words, these institutions can do what they like and get away with it - thanks to a Republican Congress and a lame –duck President.

As a former member of President Clinton's cabinet- it was Reich's responsibility to have a private audience with the President and show him the ramifications of signing this terrible Act. But at the time the President's sex scandal made him toxic and no one wanted to be around him - professionally or privately so- Mr. Reich stood by and watched.

Real History

Now I see Mr. Reich speaking and talking about economic equality and aligning himself with the Occupy Movement. From a historic standpoint, I agree with Mr. Reich's accuracy of the economic situation in America but Mr. Reich forgets that he helped shape the economic disparity when he helped push the NAFTA agreement and stood by and did nothing to stop President

Clinton from signing the Gramm-Leach-Bailey Act. It's amazing to me that a brilliant mind like Mr. Reich seemed to be absent minded about his role in this tragedy. Owe up to what you did and take some responsibility- C'mon Man!!

December 22nd

My Christmas Wish

The late journalist Eric Sevareid famously said that, *"Christmas is a necessity. There has to be at least one day of year to remind us that we're here for something else besides ourselves."* With that same spirit in mind -my Christmas wish is simple- Good will towards mankind. If we take nothing away from this holiday season we should know that if we work towards a common goal than anything is possible. Just take a look at what happened in our collective world and tell me that change is not possible. We all cry, laugh, and wish that things could be better- this is our collective history- this is our collective prayer. So my wish for the 1Lovejoy Nation is peace and joy on this holiday season. Thanks for reading.

Festival of lights. Kobe, Japan

December 29th

Is Common Sense Back In Vogue?

In the early 2000's, people in the U.S. walked around in a funk thinking that everything was going to be okay. Then two wars broke out; the U.S. housing bubble started to bust and the world economy tanked; we looked around and saw that the world was different. We uncovered the little old man controlling the lever behind the great and power OZ and we did not like it- not one bit. Then our shock and awe became self-preservation and then anger. We started groups like the Tea Party and the 99 Percent to give a voice to our frustration- we were told there was no Santa Claus and that Christmas is not coming for a long time.

Maybe the economic down turn was a good thing for the world- especially America. It got us back to living within our means and not competing with *The Jones'*. It seemed that we started to value people in our lives a little bit more and appreciated the opportunities that we are afforded. We don't take things for granted anymore (I hope).

The professional malcontents will always be disenchanted with the world because the trees aren't being hugged enough or that they need more yachts to water ski behind. It's their job to make you feel miserable and blame others for the problem. Their rants are white noise- disregard their chatter.

This blogger believes that common sense is coming back. Extremism has run its course- from religious to political- it's over. A spirit of unity and shared sacrifice must be the order of the day or we will suffer. We may not always agree with one another but we can listen to what each other has to say.

2012

"I have been driven to my knees many times by the overwhelming conviction that I had no place else to go."

– Abraham Lincoln

The Clowns Are In Town!!

This blog tries to present stories that fly under the radar of mainstream media but in this case I will make an exception. This will be the only time I will write an article about the 2012 Republican Presidential Candidates because I feel that none of these people will win the presidency- no matter how hard they try. To make my point – here is a quick summary of the candidates so far.

Mitt Romney- This is the next man for the Republican Party. The party feels that he is just moderate enough to beat President Obama in 2012. There is just one problem- no one likes him- neither his political base nor the people he used to represent in Massachusetts as Governor. He has already been labeled a flip- flopper and a member of the 1%. Furthermore, America is not ready to embrace a person of the Mormon faith. This will be his Achilles heel.

Mitt Romney is running for the presidency for all the wrong reason- the prize. He believes that if he wins that he would redeem his father's good name (His father was Governor **George Romney** of Michigan who ran for President in 1968). Just like George W. Bush- pride is what's driving him and not doing the work for the American people.

Newt Gingrich- This former House Speaker was the man who brought impeachment charges before the House of Representatives on President Clinton because of his extramarital affair with a White House intern. At the same time, this man, was having an extramarital affair with his now current wife. In other words, Newt Gingrich is a hypocrite. This single incident disqualifies this man of any leadership position. Moreover, by all accounts this man is arrogant, dismissive, and disrespectful to people who do not share his point of view. This man has so many issues that it would fill a magazine periodical from cover to cover. He is all smoke and mirrors and just like Romney he is after the prize and not about helping people.

Michele Bachman- She's just bat shit crazy.

Rick Perry- If you sound like George W. Bush, walk like him, and talk like him; you are probably going to run your administration just like him. No thanks – I'm just getting over the W. years.

Rick Santorum- He's just a male version of Michele Bachmann.

Ron Paul- this Texas Congressman is a **Libertarian** but he's running for the Republican nomination for the second time. Libertarian's believe in the doctrine of free will, and you only have to look at a third world country to see how a hands off government operates (refer to **Haiti**). With the discovery of his racist filled newsletter that disregards the Martin Luther King National Holiday and slams the Israeli state, his path is set for yet another unsuccessful run at the presidency.

Jon Huntsman- He's not ready to be President- he got talked into it. In 2016, he will be more polished and seasoned to run for the office.

The 2012 Republican Candidates are a bunch of clowns that should not be running for the highest office in the land. Their whole agenda is to repeal the new Healthcare Legislation, cut taxes for the rich, and provoke a conflict with Iran. These are the only issues that matter to them as a whole.

Most of them have no strong international/foreign policy nor do they have a concrete domestic agenda. These candidates are running on the belief that *White America* is tired of seeing a Black man in charge. If you look into all of their backgrounds most of them oppose any policy that promotes minority, women, sexual, or economic equality.

Let's say if one of them gets the nomination and they probably will choose a minority, a woman, or both to balance the ticket. It will have to be a rising star in the Republican Party; probably Governor **Nikki Haley** from South Carolina (Anglo- Indian), Senator **Mark Rubio** from Florida (Cuban), Governor **Bobby Jindal** from Louisiana (Indian) or **Herman Cain** (African-American). One of these puppets will be sent out to say the most disrespectful things about the President. They will not focus on the issues- they will focus on his race. But at the end of the day the Republican nominee will have to debate President Obama who will out debate whoever he faces. That will be the election- it will come down to the Presidential Debates.

While the media is trying to make people interested in the race for presidency, it is overwhelmingly obvious that President Obama is going to win. The Tea Party members in Congress destroyed any chance that someone from their party will win the presidency (especially with that Debt Ceiling debate). President Obama will run against Congress and he will win.

In a world in flux- this blogger doesn't want to see any of these people making any decisions for the American people. President Obama has earned my trust- the Republican Candidates have earned my scorn with their fear based politics.

January 10th

Advice for the Returning Veteran

The war in Iraq has ended and the war in Afghanistan will be over in a couple of years. This will be happy days for families and friends who love and support these brave men and women who protect and serve our country. However, there is a rude awakening when you get back and you will soon ask yourself, *"Is this the country I fought for? Are these the people I fought to protect?"* Being a former veteran myself I can identify with what you are about to go through. Here is some advice that I learnt along the way that I would like to share with my fellow veterans.

- Use your G.I. Bill and get into an accredited University because you can't have a decent job without a degree despite of what they told you in T.A.P class.
- Use the VA benefits that you are owed. It will be hard to obtain but keep fighting to get what is rightfully yours.
- Keep a copy of your DD-214 form. This is the most important paper you will receive.
- Travel and see some part of the world that is not affected by war.
- Don't pick-up bad habits or pick-up new ones. At this stage of the game you need to be focused.
- Do a follow-up on everything. In the civilian world- a lack of effort is painfully obvious.

- No one will be able to understand what you went through or saw, so try to keep in contact with a military buddy that you served with. It can make the transition to civilian life a little easier if you have someone to talk to.
- Don't take your frustration out on your loved ones- they don't deserve that. Try to find an activity to focus your attention on.
- Don't feel ashamed of your service but don't boast about it either. You're beginning a new chapter in your life and your military service is just one of them.
- Get ready for rejection. Employers are afraid to hire veterans. Thus, going back to school is a good idea.
- Don't get involved with political or nonprofits organizations because they will use you and spit you out after they exploit your military service for their own gain.
- Don't believe in all these so-called Patriots. You are the true patriot- don't ever forget that.
- Don't get frustrated in the workplace. The lack of getting the job done in a day compared to doing everything at the last minute makes no sense. Deal with it and move on.

The transition into civilian life can be overwhelming at times but keep your military bearing about you- you'll be okay. Remember, you just got back from a combat zone – you can take on whatever situation comes your way. Make a plan, stick to the plan and execute. There will be many pitfalls along the way- it's how you pick yourself up that will tell what you are made of. Trust yourself and you'll should be okay.

January 12th

We're Sorry Dr. King

In the United States, on the 3rd Monday in January, the country celebrates the legacy of Dr. Martin Luther King Jr. This one man helped shape the America most people around the world recognize today. Without him- civil rights for minorities and women would go unrecognized. In other words- the United States would have still been an apartheid country. He believed that nonviolent resistance should expose unjust laws and the corruption in government systems; he believed that a person should be judged by the content of their character and not their race; he believed in economic equality and a fair share at the American way of life. However, in this country today, we take for granted the liberties that he fought so hard to achieve for all Americans.

Origins

When Dr. King was asked to lead the civil rights struggle he hesitated. He knew that his life, as well as the life of his family would be in danger. With humility, he accepted the role and pushed forward to advance the cause of civil rights. The message he presented was simple- he wanted the government to honor the U.S. Constitution and keep the promise they made when the former slaves were emancipated. It's that simple. Keep your promise. However, in today's America, promises are being broken and laws are being rewritten to keep the status quo.

Current Protest Movements

The recent protest movements in America seem to have an air of selfishness about them and a secret agenda to express individual views and opinions. These groups take advantage of the frustration of individuals who don't know what to do and need someone to blame. With all these protests, I do not see nor do I hear a concrete plan to change a thing. No new ideas have come to the forefront- only recycled ideas that pit one against the other, keeping the rich man rich and the poor man poor and everyone else stuck in the middle. These protests are not changing anything but making things worse.

Apology

Dr. King, on behave of all Americans, I would like to apologize for not heeding your message of working together to find a solution to problems. I apologize for people not realizing the tremendous contribution you made in the world because they can't get past their racist ideology. I apologize for the people in your era that were supposed to be stewards of your struggle but shunned their responsibility. I apologize that young people don't realize what the struggle brings and that change takes time. For all of them I'm sorry and I hope in the near future we can live up to your example.

The **Martin Luther King, Jr. Memorial** at Yerba Buena Gardens

25 Books That Shaped America

The author Thomas C. Foster has written a book called *Twenty-five Books That Shaped America*. While reading this book I agreed with some selections. However, I disagreed with about 75% of them. I don't think the author took into account that the books that changed America should be transformative and not personal favorites. The criteria should be based on whether authors provoke social or philosophical change in the way we American's view ourselves. Without further ado, here is the 1Lovejoy's list.

1- Invisible Man – Ralph Ellison
2- Uncle Tom's Cabin- Harriet Beecher Stowe
3- To Kill A Mockingbird- Harper Lee
4- In Cold Blood- Truman Capote
5- Rights of Man- Thomas Paine
6- The Federalist Papers- Alexander Hamilton, James Madison, and John Jay
7- Grapes of Wrath- John Steinbeck
8- The Jungle-Uptown Sinclair
9- The Great Gatsby- F. Scott Fitzgerald
10- The Old Man and the Sea- Ernest Hemingway
11- The Murders in the Rue Morgue- Edgar Allen Poe
12- The Scarlett Letter- Nathaniel Hawthorne
13- Native Son- Richard Wright
14- A Thin Red Line-James Jones
15- Letters from a Birmingham Jail- Dr. Martin Luther King Jr.
16- Profile In Courage- John F. Kennedy
17- Dreams From My Father- Barack Obama
18- I Know Why The Cage Birds Sing- Dr. Maya Angelou
19- Interpreter of Maladies- Jhumpa Lahiri
20- Post Office- Charles Bukowski
21- On the Road- Jack Kerouac
22- Roots- Alex Haley
23- Walden- Henry David Thoreau
24- The Autobiography of Miss Jane Pittman- Ernest Gaines
25- The Wealth of Nations- Adam Smith

City Lights Bookshop. San Francisco, CA

January 26th

Random Acts of Kindness

In today's cynical world, human beings view each other with a bit of suspicion. We believe that everyone has an agenda and would do anything to achieve their ultimate objective. Is this that type of society we've become? Is this the kind of society we want? I think we can do better than the path we're on at this present time because I found a solution to the problem- random acts of kindness.

The act of random kindness happens when you're helpful or courteous to your fellow human being. Hopefully, this will start a chain reaction that forces people subconsciously to show a bit of kindness to each other. This activity is simple and it's free. For example, opening the door for an elderly person or giving directions to someone (if you know the way). Again, it's free and easy and takes very little time to do.

1Lovejoy Nation, let's start a meme. Let's get as many people to start this revolution of being responsible for one another; let's start a revolution of doing and saying the right things; let's start with looking in the mirror and saying, *"What can I do today to make the world better?"* I think we are all tired of the fighting and finger pointing. Let us —as human beings- treat each other with a little respect.

February 9th

Jim Crow All Over Again: The America's Cup

In the so called progressive city of San Francisco, the Golden Gate Yacht Club (GGYC), defender of the coveted America's Cup (International regatta) rejected an African- American sailing team's right to compete as a defender candidate.

On December 12th, a lawsuit was filed in New York City that alleges America's Cup organizers are in breach of trustee duties by self – dealing and discrimination of persons to participate. The lawsuit was filed on behalf of the African Diaspora Maritime (ADM), a nonprofit organization founded by sea captain Charles Kithcart based in North Carolina. *"The lawsuit alleges that GGYC ignored Kithcart's repeated requests to be considered for entry into the competition almost until the deadline last spring, then rejected ADM on an arbitrary and unequal basis compared with the treatment of other competitors."*

The GGYC accepted, then rejected, and later refunded ADM's $25,000 application fee. The GGYC claim that they were not satisfied that the nonprofit would have the necessary resources to compete. Furthermore, they said, *"that the GGYC would only accept those it is satisfied having the necessary resources... and experience to have a reasonable chance of winning the America's Cup Defender Series."*

Despite the GGYC's concerns- Mr. Kithcart seemed to have everything in place. Mr. Kithcart's ADM sailing team includes African- American Olympian sailors; a well-known Rhode Island yacht designer –David Pedrick who designed America's Cup racing yachts and monetary funding. Mr. Kithcart hopes to raise additional funds by *"creating a groundswell with the public"*. However, America's Cup historian John Rousmaniere believes that since the GGYC has not invited other U.S. yacht clubs to compete that they will invoke their rights under the "Deed of Gift." The Deed of Gift states that GGYC is under no obligation to accept the rights of other American teams to compete as defenders.

With all this uncertainty, Mr. Kilhcart is confident that he will compete in the America's Cup and challenge the U.S. Team Oracle in the Defender Cup Series. The sea captain said it best:

"ADM's mission is to train African-American youth as competitive sailors, cultivate youth interest in math and science as applied to nautical skill, and make a splash on the world stage by breaking into a predominantly white sport with a black-led team, a 'la the Jamaican bobsledders from the film Cool Running."

As it is, in the American-American experience - just another barrier to breakthrough. Good Luck to you Captain!!

Hoisting the sail on San Francisco Bay, San Francisco CA

The Great Migration Back to the South

In American History, The Great Migration is the period from World War 1 to the 1970's when African-Americans moved to the industrializing North to escape prejudice and find work. Nowadays, many African–Americans who are young and college educated are heading back to the American South to live. Cities like Atlanta, Miami, and Dallas are all prime destinations for this group of people who see more opportunities in the south for work and to enjoy a quality of life that was not afforded in the East and the Midwest at this point in time. A demographer said, *"The percentage of blacks leaving big cities in the East and in the Midwest and heading to the South is now at the highest levels in decades."*

Some blacks say they are leaving not only to find jobs, but also because they have soured on race relations. Candace Wilkins, a 27 year old business degree graduate who has plans to move to Charlotte, North Carolina from St. Albans, New York said it best," *My grandmother's generation left the South and came to the North to escape segregation and racism. Now, I'm going back because New York has become like the old South in its racial attitudes."*

Many African-Americans see the New South as a place where one can actually afford a home; send their kids to safer schools; reconnect with their spiritual roots, and have a quality of life that can be achieved. With the Great Recession, came an awakening for many African-Americans that you can always come home again!!

The Importance of the Separation of Church and State

In 1802, Thomas Jefferson wrote a letter to the Danbury Baptist Association about the *"walls of the separation of church and state"*. Jefferson wrote the following," ... *I contemplate with sovereign reverence that act of the whole American people which declared that their legislature should 'make no law respecting an establishment of religion, or prohibiting the free exercise thereof,' thus building a wall of separation between Church & State."*

In this eloquent statement, Jefferson reemphasized that in the First Amendment of the U.S. Constitution that church and state should remain separate at all cost. This doctrine served this country well for over 200 years. Recently, Republican presidential candidate Rick Santorum- in reference to the 1960's presidential candidate, Senator John F. Kennedy's speech about the separation of church and state statement- made a comment that would make a Constitutionalist squirm. Senator Kennedy had stated, *"I believe in an America where the separation of church and state is absolute."* Mr. Santorum on the other hand comments, *"There are things that triggered the privatization of faith and I think that's a bad thing."* He goes on to say that, *"he wanted more of a role for people of faith in public life than Kennedy had outlined"*.

After critics from secular and religious organizations slammed him for his statements, Mr. Santorum quickly backtracked and said he regretted his comments. I believe Mr. Santorum's comments came from a place of ignorance and fear and he might need a history refresher when it comes to religious run states.

Theocratic State

In our world, Theocratic States are the most corrupt and backward societies. The lack of education opportunities for all their citizens and the mistreatment of women is shocking and appalling. We have only to look at our recent history when the U.S. and their NATO allies invaded Afghanistan and toppled the Taliban after the attacks of 9/11. That society harkens back to the middle ages but Afghanistan is now making its way back to integrate with a modern society were everyone can have an education and their women can feel empowered. Repression is the hallmark of theocratic regimes.

Analysis

I believe Mr. Santorum was addressing right-wing religious nuts who believe that the church should be involved in the decision making process of the U.S. government. This notion is simply dangerous and naive. We have only to look at history to see how long a Theocratic State stays in power and that's not for long. I know Mr. Santorum is trying to fire-up his base but in the long-term, do you really want to be beholden to these people?

March 6th

War Fatigue

President Obama met with Israel's Prime Minister Benjamin Netanyahu for talks about Iran's nuclear program. It seems that Israel wants to destroy Iran's nuclear facilities by military action. On the other hand, the U.S. wants more time for economic sanctions to take effects. If Israel takes any sort of action against Iran it would force the U.S. to support Israel because of their alliance. This position puts the Obama administration at odds with the Israeli government wanting to start yet another conflict in the region that the U.S. would be forced into.

The American public is war fatigued. The support for wanting to go into the Middle East again is at best, minimal. Americans trust the Obama administration to handle U.S. foreign policy because compared to the last administration diplomacy is the first line of defense. Lest we forget that the U.S. went into the Iraq War with half-truths and misinformation about *Weapons of Mass Destruction* (WMD).

Throughout Mr. Netanyahu's political career, he has always been a hawk about military matters, i.e. shoot now and ask questions later. The Prime

Minister needs to take a deep breath and let the process take its course. Rushing into a situation like this costs lives, money, resources and produces more enemies. It would be more prudent to let the economic sanctions take effect and gather more information about Iran's nuclear program. If these actions fail, then destroying Iran's nuclear facilities would be permissible because Israel would have the moral high ground for wanting to protect themselves and the world. Any other unjustified action will label Israel as warmongers.

March 8th

Limbaugh's Fluke

Every once in a great while this blog congratulates an individual for standing up to the powers that be and this is one of those times. Ms. Sandra Fluke is a Georgetown University law student who was asked to testify before a U.S. House committee about U.S. health insurance. The *1Lovejoy Nation* would like to thank Ms. Fluke who dared to disagree with conservative talk show host Rush Limbaugh over the issue of contraceptive mandates and the right to free access to those products.

After Ms. Fluke's testimony, Limbaugh took to his radio show and made a few comments about her. Limbaugh said, *"She wants to be paid to have sex. She's having so much sex she can't afford contraception. She wants you and me and the taxpayers to pay for her"*.

With these comments, Limbaugh nailed his own coffin. People were outraged which caused advertisers to pull their sponsorship from his radio show and countless women's organizations are targeting Limbaugh for his ignorance.

With this firestorm ablaze, you knew that Rush was going to make an apology and hoped that the situation would go away. However, Ms. Fluke didn't accept his apology. She said that his apology was *"insufficient"*.

Over the years, Rush Limbaugh has managed to upset everyone who is not rich and white. However, it took insulting a young woman who wanted other women to have free access to healthcare. Let's hope that this serves as a warning to neo-conservatives.

March 15ᵗʰ

What The Fuck Is Up With Gas Prices?

Around the world, the price of fuel seems to be going up every day. The main reason for this price markup is the rumors of war and the mass media's effort to fuel the fire. Oil speculators are betting that Israel will strike Iran's nuclear facilities in the near future. Also, they know that Iran is trying to block the Straits of Hormuz where most of the oil traffic is located. With all this developments in the Middle East region no wonder oil speculators are jumping for joy. It's like the Iraq War all over again.

Many people are blaming world leaders for high fuel prices. We as uninformed citizens forget that world leaders can only do so much about this situation. We have only to look in the mirror to find the real collaborators- it is us. Our addiction to fossil fuels is driving up the price and funding third world dictatorships who then dictate terms to the world. We are addicted to fuel and if we don't find a way to curb our addiction then the oil speculators and third world dictators will keep on driving up the prices and you'll have to take it.

However, it's not too late. We can become better stewards of this earth by respecting her. Let us support ongoing research to find alternatives to fossil fuel. Let's support politicians and researchers in their efforts to try to find a solution to this problem, if we don't, higher fuel prices are here to stay or until the oil runs dry.

March 27th

The Inevitable Scandal

Is it just me or does it feel like an inevitable scandal is in the future of the 2012 Republican's Presidential Candidates Mitt Romney and Rick Santorum? Both men claim to be devoted to their religious faith; both men claim to have loving marriages; both men seem to be straight laced and uptight; all indications lead to one of them having a big skeleton in their closet.

I wonder what inevitable scandal will take down one (or maybe both) of these guys?

1) **Sex Scandal**- Old Fashioned and a favorite of the Republican establishment.

2) **Homosexual Sex Scandal**- These men are religiously oppressed-right?

3) **Gaffe**- Nothing like insulting women, minorities and homosexuals to get you elected.

4) **Stealing Campaign Funds**- Nothing like stealing from the same people that gave you money.

5) **Sex Tape Scandal**- Do you really want to see any of these guys "*get their groove on*"?

6) **Dancing With the Stars Scandal**- Please, don't make them dance!!

As you can see the Republican contest is so boring that I had to think of some way to make this contest between these boring men interesting. It's like looking at the same guy except one is Mormon and the other is a Catholic.

As I said in the beginning of the year- this contest was over before it even started. See you guys in 2016.

April 4th

Strip Search Everyone

A few days ago, the U.S. Supreme Court voted in a 5-4 decision (Chief Justice Anthony M. Kennedy was the swing vote and went along with the conservatives on the court) to make it legal for officials to strip search anyone who is arrested – no matter how minor the offense - before admitting them to jail. So, if a person is unable to pay a parking fine, they will be arrested, then strip searched, and thrown in jail to serve out their allotted time.

This case came about because of a New Jersey man named Albert W. Florence. In 2005, *"Mr. Florence was in the passenger seat of his BMW when a state trooper pulled his wife, April, over for speeding. A records search revealed an outstanding warrant for Mr. Florence's arrest based on an unpaid fine. (The information was wrong; the fine had been paid.) Mr. Florence was held for a week in jails in Burlington and Essex Counties, and he was strip-searched in each. There is some dispute about the details, but general agreement that he was made to stand naked in front of a guard who required him to move intimate parts of his body. The guards did not touch him."*

Many human rights organizations are outraged at the decision. Ten states (along with the Federal Government) forbid these strip search tactics that the U.S. Supreme Court just approved. The Supreme Court *"did not say that strip-searches of every new arrestee were required; it ruled, rather, that the Fourth Amendment's prohibition of unreasonable searches did not forbid them."*

This ruling shows how important voting in elections is. The Justices who voted for strip searches were selected by Republican Presidents. Those who voted against were chosen by Democratic Presidents. Elections are a fight about ideologies and the Supreme Court is the ultimate legacy for any President who wishes to leave their mark in the American lexicon. This ruling is proof.

April 18th

Nazis In Congress

Recently, the American Nazi Party registered a lobbyist in Washington D.C. on Capitol Hill. This will give the group unprecedented access to members of Congress to influence their views on particular issues. The leader of this effort John Bowles, 55, said *"his official status as a lobbyist was something the 53-year-old party planned to "try out for the first time and see if it flies."* He goes on to say, *"I'm not going to go in and shove a swastika in their face,".....I use a very careful and objective approach. There might be some congressmen who crumple up the paper and some who say 'this is interesting."*

The silver lining to this whole issue is to see which members of Congress would consort with this lobby group and would seriously consider their views valid. But let's be real for a moment, this group should have never been allowed to form a lobby. This group is a homegrown terrorist organization and they are no better than Al-Qaeda. Their organization has committed hate crimes on minorities, immigrants and people with alternative lifestyles. To grant them access to Congress is a slap in the face to people who fought for civil and human rights for everyone.

This blog urges the ACLU and the U.S. Justice Department to investigate this matter because if the government allows this to go on, I see no end in sight to all of the fringe groups who will try to breach the halls of Congress.

May 9th

The Great Student Loan Debt Debate

President Obama is in a fight with the Republican controlled Congress over Student Loan debt. The issue is that by July 1st interest rates will double from 3.4% to 6.8%. This will happen because the 2007 College Cost Reduction and Access Act, which reduced interest rates on subsidized Stafford loans, will expire. Republicans in Congress feel that extending the low rates would be too costly and would be a burden to millions of taxpayers.

The Real Issue

The real issue is not about student loans. The real issue is about the Republican Party protecting their interest by not raising taxes on the wealthiest American. Once again, the Republican ideology of trickle-down economics rears its ugly head. This party would rather put the burden on people who are trying to make their way through college, than tax some fat cat on Wall Street. Their strategy is to use the debt issue to suit their agenda. Have we forgotten, that the Republicans patron saint, Ronald Reagan himself stated that, 'national debt doesn't matter'.

Conclusion

This is the same reason why the Occupy Movement had so much momentum. Young people know they will pay double on a bill they can't afford while they see bankers, hedge-fund managers, and Wall Street paying little to no taxes. If the Republican controlled Congress allows this bill to expire they lose any chance of winning back the White House let alone Congress. The youth vote counts.

May 23rd

In Yo' Face (book), Saverin

Ahead of Facebook's massive initial public offering last week, the company's co-founder Eduardo Saverin decided to give up his U.S. citizenship and live in Singapore. It's believed that Mr. Saverin is giving up his citizenship to avoid paying capital gain tax. It just so happens, that Singapore does not have a capital gain tax so this move could save Mr. Saverin anywhere from 67 to a 100 million dollars.

When Democratic lawmakers found out what Mr. Saverin was doing they were furious. To close the loophole in the system, Senator Chuck Schumer

(New York-D) and Senator Bob Casey (Pennsylvania-D) are introducing a bill in Congress that would heavily penalize anyone trying to avoid paying taxes. *"Under their legislation, any American who renounces his or her citizenship for the purpose of avoiding taxes will be punished in two ways: They will be barred from re-entering the U.S., and their future investments in the U.S. will be taxed at a 30 percent rate."* Both Senator's wrote this bill to try to stop this "despicable trend."

This blogger would like to congratulate Senator Schumer and Casey for finally recognizing what's been going on for the last 30 years and writing a concrete bill that addresses this issue. It's shameful that Mr. Saverin gave up his citizenship not because of political or moral reasons. He gave it up for greed and avarice. Mr. Saverin should never be allowed back into the U.S. – ever!

May 30th

Defend New Orleans: Volume 2

Last week, Advance Publication (owned by the Newhouse Family of New York) decided that the New Orleans newspaper- Times Picayune- will be distributed only 3 times a week (Wednesday, Friday and Sunday). The company wants to focus more on the web publication and lay off staff to make a leaner product. In other words, it's cheaper to manage a website and lay off employees because there is more money to be made.

Bucking the Trend

In the last couple of years, many newspapers have gone away. Let's face it, print is dead. However, the Times Picayune is in a different category. Most people in the city (unfortunately) do not have access to the web or are unwilling to learn how to access the technology. The tradition of picking up the paper and going to a favorite breakfast spot, barber shop or café -talking about what's going on in City Hall or if the Saints or L.S.U. is going to win a championship - is a daily occurrence. The Times Picayune is how the city of

New Orleans becomes a community, because everyone has access to the same information.

Intervention

To stop the plans of the Newhouse family, a small group of local citizens have offered to buy the paper. Alas, the Newhouse's are refusing the offer because they want to stay in the New Orleans market.

The Importance of the "Pic"

Since Hurricane Katrina, The Times Picayune has been a vital source of information. People who were relocated found comfort in the written words of insightful reporting on the post-Katrina experience. To take the dailies away, to experiment with a format that worked in Ann Arbor, Michigan will either transform or eliminate the newspaper altogether.

The Newhouse's are one of the wealthiest families in the country and do not need the money. It is ego and advertising dollars that is driving this decision. Now, the city of New Orleans does not claim to be New York City or San Francisco with residents numbering into the millions. People have to realize that New Orleans was almost destroyed and it will take a little while for this truly original American city to come back to full strength. The Times Picayune is a steady institution that keeps citizens informed about the progress and mishaps of the city. I'm afraid this will be gone if the newspaper is not run daily. The people's watchdog will be diminished.

Saturday Edition of The Times-Picayune, New Orleans LA

June 6th

Eliminate Student Debt

With the rising cost of higher education in the United States (and the world) it is time to ask ourselves - should student debt be eliminated? The reason why this question should be raised is because there seems to be an effort to make college graduates in debt to lending institutions before they can succeed in the pursuit of their chosen profession. In this essay, we will examine why student debt should be forgiven and find reasonable solutions of how the debt should be paid off.

The Problem

Think back to the time you were 17/ 18 years old. Life was carefree and everything seemed possible. If someone older told you to sign a document that you were told to sign- then you did- because you thought they were looking out for your best interest. Furthermore, at that age, you don't even know what an interest rate is. Now, fast forward four years later and six months after graduation when you're handed a massive bill and told that you have to pay it back. In your mind, you know you never borrowed that much money. That's when you realize what an interest rate is all about. Now you're thrust into a world of financial chaos.

The scenario that I just explained is what millions of people who went to college/university face. For a banking institution to shove a piece of paper in a kid's face and tell them to sign on the dotted line or they won't be able to go to school is cruel and dangerously close to extortion. This kind of financial terrorism has to stop.

The Solution

Since University/College Presidents are beholden to rich alumni and boosters they will do nothing to help. This is why the federal government needs to step in and become a mediator in this process. The federal government needs to assure that the interest rate is low or at a reasonable rate so that students have a chance of repaying the loan; or if a student is unable to pay the loan then options are available so that the loan obligations can be met. For example:

- *Student must serve two years of military service.*
- *Student must serve two years in a federally run community based program.*
- *Student (if a Doctor or Lawyer) must provide two years of free services to the under privileged.*

If a student chooses any one of these options – then the federal government will pay the banks back on behalf of the student. This way the banks, the student(s), college/universities, federal government and the community at large would win.

The Bottom Line

The solution to this problem is fairly simple; if a student is unable to pay back their loan then there are options that are available for them. The solutions presented in this essay are hopefully the start of a more meaningful dialogue that needs to be addressed. If the banks received a bailout-shouldn't the people who are going to shape the future deserve that same right? I think so.

Calapalooza- UC Berkeley's annual student-activity fair

July 4th

Happy Birthday America

Being an American, I can make corny clichés about how God blessed America with tons of land, wealth and people. It's the obvious things to say. However, I just want to say to the rest of the world that America is still a young country and still learning how to be a super power. We're not perfect but what country is?

Moreover, I would like to apologize to the world for the years 2000 through 2008 (George W. Bush's presidency). Sorry about that. It seemed that my fellow countrymen/women got carried away and wanted to secure the remaining available fossil fuel in the Middle East for our country before the world supply ran dry. I guess that's what happens when you put an oil man in office. So to make peace with the world we gave you our current President- Mr. Obama. You're welcome.

America, even with all its hypocrisy and malcontents, where one can disagree with another person and not be killed or blacklisted because of their beliefs, where a person with the will to make their own destiny can succeed. However, here's a warning you may want to heed about the American dream- read the fine print! Happy Birthday- America.

July 4th festivities at Jack London Square. Oakland, CA

It's Official... No One Likes Mitt Romney

In early July, House Speaker John Boehner attended a political fundraiser in West Virginia. Mr. Boehner was asked a simple question *"Can you make me love Mitt Romney?"* The House Speaker responded: *"No, we're just politicians. I wasn't elected to play God. The American people probably aren't going to fall in love with Mitt Romney."*

If that wasn't bad enough, Mr. Romney was booed and heckled at the NAACP annual meeting for saying he can do a better job for black people than Mr. Obama. And the gaffe machine kept rolling overseas when he criticized the London Olympic Committee and angered Palestinians by using racist and insensitive comments. It's amazing, Mr. Romney has managed to be disliked by his political base (Republicans) and has also managed to gaffe his way overseas and is disliked there as well. Not even on George W. Bush's worst day has he pissed off so many people in a short amount of time.

In America, people need to like their President. It doesn't matter what political party they are affiliated with but the President must be a person that commands respect from his friends and foes alike. To put it quiet bluntly- Mr. Romney doesn't have those qualities. As this blog stated in January, Mr. Romney seeks the presidency for the prize. He is not about the work of bringing communities together and in his opinion they can fend for themselves.

This election cycle reminds me of the 1996 Presidential race that pitted Senator Bob Dole against President Clinton. Everyone knew the outcome but were too afraid to tell Mr. Dole. Fast forward to the present and we are at that same crossroad. The mass media need to stop giving Mr. Romney and his campaign false hope. The Republican Party needs to gear up for the 2016 election when the economy will be robust and their candidate will have a real chance at winning. This candidate is tailor made to be the sacrificial lamb for all Republicans. This presidential race was over when it started. No matter how much Super Pac money you throw at the problem being likeable counts, especially if you're going to lead the free world.

August 22ⁿᵈ

The End of Racism

Immediately after the election of President Obama, the first African–American ever to serve in the highest office, most people in the mass media cried that it was *the end of racism*. On the other hand many minorities in the U.S. believed that this statement was a bit naïve.

The country's identity is rooted in racial, gender and blue blood politics. Just because an African-American was elected President doesn't erase over 200 years of deep rooted so-called tradition passed on from one generation to the next. We have only to look at the 2008 Presidential electoral map and see how deeply rooted that belief system runs. This belief system masks itself in Christianity, private social clubs and organizations and act as havens for people who would like to believe in a pastime paradise and wish for the good ole' days.

Electoral Map Wikipedia.org

Defend New Orleans: Volume 3

Hurricane Isaac is taking a similar path that Hurricane Katrina did 7 years ago. Hurricane Isaac is also disrupting a Republican National Convention just as Hurricane Gustav did 4 years ago. This hurricane is a reminder to the nation of the failure of the Bush 43rd Administration and state and local leaders. Thankfully, this time, all phases of government appear to be working for the greater good.

The Republican Convention

Within a span of 4 years, it appears that another hurricane is raining on the Republican's parade. Hurricane Isaac is approaching the city of New Orleans on the anniversary of Hurricane Katrina and the nation can't help but be reminded of the tragedy that Hurricane Katrina spawned. It showed that when a person in office is aloof then the constituents are in trouble. This latest convention is just a reminder of what Republicans tend to do in situations like these- keep the party going and worry about the little people later.

Attitude of the City

The city is taking their cue from Mayor Mitch Landrieu. The Mayor is betting that the new and improved levee system will hold. Citizens seem to share in his optimism. Most people in New Orleans believe that the storm will pass them by or be weaker than most experts are predicting. You can see their optimism in the provisions they are collecting- water, perishable food items, party favors and plenty of alcohol. These *Hurricane Parties* are a reminder of Pre- Katrina and a belief that the city has seen the worst that Mother Nature has unleashed upon them. Let's hope that the Mayor is correct in his optimism- for the people's sake.

Resilient Spirit

Once again this truly American city has caught the world's attention. This time the nation and the world is waiting to see if all phases of government have gotten their act together; waiting to see how people will respond; hoping for the best but bracing for the worst. This is what everyone is waiting to see. Speaking for myself and all New Orleanians- we will defend New Orleans. We will show that unique American trait called *Grit*. Good or bad- we are ready to show the world what we are made of once again. This time- we're ready.

Jackson Square. New Orleans, LA

A Review of the Republican National Convention

The essay will be a review of the Republican National Convention. I will also do the same for the Democratic National Convention next week. This will be an honest assessment of how an ordinary American citizen views the direction and vision of each party. Let's start with the Republicans.

Appearance & Message

The Republican National Convention reminds me of a private country club that only allows one or two minorities to say that they are all inclusive. This convention also reminds me that angry white men want to be in total control. Over and over, lies sprinkled with a bit of the truth were the mantle for speeches. A number of news organizations fact checked their statements and found discrepancies. This party was selling the idea that America is not better off under the Obama Administration. I guess the Republicans consider these facts a failure; adverting another Great Depression, leading the U.S. out of two wars honorably, killing Osama bin Laden, aiding Libya rebels in the liberation of their county, restructuring of FEMA, saving the U.S. auto industry, passing Mortgage reform, eliminating the don't ask /don't tell military policy, passing affordable health care and pushing through compressive immigration legislation. All this while having an obstructionist Republican Congress fighting him every step of the way.

The Highlight

However, the highlight of the convention was not the vice presidential nominee Paul Ryan's speech nor the Republican presidential nominee Mitt Romney. The focus was on actor/director and former mayor of Carmel, California- Clint Eastwood. His rant about a chair and that crazy speech seemed to be all over the place. It was funny and disturbing at the same time. But maybe that's how the Republican Party really is- a confused angry old white man that has diarrhea of the mouth with no clue of what's really going on.

Insensitive

When Hurricane Isaac was pounding the Gulf Coast region- no real heartfelt response was shown. It appeared that the delegates and the politicos were annoyed that Mother Nature was disturbing their party.

Summary

In a nutshell, the Republican National Convention shows the American people who they are, people who will start wars/conflicts, cut taxes for the wealthiest among us; privatize or outsource all Medicare and Medicaid programs; reverse Roe v. Wade and repeal the new Healthcare law. The Republican platform is the same ole' ideology and they don't realize that the face of America is changing. That philosophy went out the door with George W. Bush. It's time for this party to reboot itself.

September 12th

A Review of the Democratic National Convention

This essay will be a review of the Democratic National Convention. This will be an honest assessment of how an ordinary American citizen views the direction and vision of the party. Without further ado- here are the Democrats.

Appearance & Message

The theme of the Democratic National Convention was that of Fear, Hope and Unity. Fear that the extreme voices of the Republican Party will continue to control Congress and possibly the White House. Hope, that the President can fulfill his campaign promises of 2008. Unity, because the fringe groups in the Democratic Party finally realized that all their agendas are at stake if the Republicans win this election.

The Highlights

The highlights of the convention were the speeches given by the First Lady Michelle Obama, former President Bill Clinton and President Obama. Each speech had a specific purpose in depth and scope. The First Lady presented President Obama as the embodiment of the American dream and how he can relate to the pain and frustration of the common man. She also humanized her husband and gave a glimpse of the true character of the man.

Not to be outdone, President Clinton gave a brilliant political speech in support of President Obama. He totally deconstructed and blew-up the Republicans argument at every level. He did what no other politician was able to do-put in laymen terms what the Republican and Democratic strategies really are. President Clinton presented his case to the American public like he was Atticus Finch defending the virtue of responsible government. From a political perspective, it was a pleasure to watch a true master at work.

Finally, it was President Obama's turn to reintroduce himself to the American people from candidate Obama to now President of the United States. He appealed to the masses to stick with him after cleaning up the economic chaos created by the prior administration. His face looked of a man that had been pushed to his limits but remained steely in his resolve. President Obama describes what hardships he faced by quoting another President – Abraham Lincoln, "*I have been driven to my knees many times by the overwhelming conviction that I had no place else to go.*" I believe in that moment people were persuaded that this man truly was thinking about the people he served.

Summary

The Democratic National Convention was an evolution of fear, hope and then unity. The Democratic Party and the American people had to be reminded of the perils the country (and the world) faced when Mr. Obama took over the presidency. These speeches reminded people that America is making positive strides again. The Democratic Party wants America to look FORWARD.

Good Luck India

Recently, the Indian government announced that the British retailer Tesco and the American retailer Wal-Mart will be allowed to open operations in the subcontinent. Both companies agree to purchase over 50% of items from the local vendors to sell in their respective stores. This move by the Indian government shows that the country has a strong middle-class and is ready to compete with the west. However, this blogger thinks this is a miscalculation by the Indian government.

Lesson from America

The company Wal-Mart has single handily ruined American small business in rural communities. Once thriving businesses were gobbled up by the mammoth that is Wal-Mart because Wal-Mart lowered their price to drive out the competition. Once the competition is eliminated - the company is able to charge whatever price they deem fair. The cruel part of this scenario is that the same small business owner(s) has to beg Wal-Mart for a job just to survive.

Wal-Mart is eying major urban areas but most community leaders /organizers in these urban areas have seen the damage Wal-Mart has brought to rural communities and are fighting the company every step of the way. This blogger can't speak about Tesco, but I've seen firsthand the power Wal-Mart wheeled and it wasn't pretty.

Summary

With the opening of these retail giants there will be a disappearance of the local vendor. Gone will be the days of bargaining for a deal; gone are the days knowing the guy that will give you a great price for fabric; gone are the days of the sights, sounds and smells of the markets. Those days will forever be gone now that Wal-Mart and Tesco are taking over. Say *"Hello"* to progress.

Indian Pothole Cover. San Francisco, CA.

September 26th

Voting Against Your Own Self Interest

This weekend, I was reminded of why I decided to walk away from the political game while I was still sane. I hope this essay will illuminate the kind rationalization some people use to justify their point of view. As strange and hypocritical as it may be, there are people in America that think this way.

The Statement

An ex-colleague made a comment that was simply shocking. He said that," *The Republican Party wouldn't be so bad if they got rid of all the right-wing extremist.*" Please note that he is gay. When I heard that statement it sent a chill down my spine. This gay man was talking about the same party who railed against homosexuality and who believed that AIDS was the "*gay cancer*". The same party who refused funding and acknowledgement for HIV/AIDS research; the same party who railed against the LGBT community for serving their country in the military and don't believe in same sex marriages-that Republican Party.

Then I realized that he was brought up in the Mid-West and that for years he was beaten over the head with Fox News propaganda. Also, he was born in the 80's. He was unaware of the rise of the Moral Majority and their medieval ideals. Then I came to the conclusion (in my personal experience) that most white males in America would vote against their own self-interest.

The People and their Rationalization

Full disclosure- I ran into these people all the time in my former line of work. Their pocket book didn't match with their beliefs. Let's be frank for a moment- the Republican Party is considered the white man's party and the people I encountered think that this party is going to look out for them. The reality is that the Republican Party lookout for those who are rich and wouldn't give a damn if you are poor and white. They use fear to gain power and make their wealthy friends even wealthier.

The people who are likely to vote for a conservative/Republican is the farmer who needs government subsidies to keep their family farm; the laid off autoworker who receives unemployment benefits because their job was outsourced overseas; the retiree who needs their Social Security check and Medicare benefits just to have a decent quality of life; the disabled veteran who needs their check and treatment from the VA just to get by. Most of these people whom I described have no trouble voting for a conservative/ Republican believing that that the government shouldn't intervene in one's personal life. They fail to see that receiving benefits, subsidies and Medicare assistance is possible because of a Democratic government in your life.

The Choice

So white men, it comes down to a simple choice, vote for your own self-interest or vote for the same Republican Party that will use sunshine patriotism to get you to ignore the real issues that affect your life. However, you should look in the mirror and blame yourself for not using your head but going to the slaughter with the rest of the sheep. The choice is yours.

October 3rd

For What It's Worth

The world is in a state of transition. On one hand, you have those who would like to continue conflicts to mask the real trouble facing their respective countries and on the other hand, you have those who are willing to face the problem head on and try to find a solution.

The Issue

The Euro Zone's financial meltdown is affecting world markets. The chickens have come home to roost and we can either deal with the issue or just kick the can down the road. Some of our public servants are willing to take these issues head on and are willing to take a hit politically because it's the right thing to do. Others avoid issues altogether and try to blame some person or a group for the problem. Believe it or not- this *"blame game"* strategy seems to work when politicos can't accept responsibility for their stewardship.

For what it's worth- we as human beings need to start looking in the mirror and accept some responsibility for what goes on in our lives and the people we elect to govern. For the most part we are transitioning from wartime to a stable economy. The issues that were kicked down the road have to be dealt with. The burden can be dumped on the middle-class and the poor to pay for past wars and infrastructure improvement or we can place the burden on the wealthy individuals and corporations that have benefited from a wartime economy. But the reality is that if wealthy individuals and corporations get a majority of the tax burden- they will pass it down to the rest of us by making products and services more expensive. That's just the honest truth.

Solution

So what to do? I hope that an old fashioned notion of *shared responsibility* comes back in vogue, one which encourages human beings to be responsible for one another. There is a verse in the bible from Matthew 25:45 that sums up this point when Jesus Christ said, *"Then he will answer them with the words, 'Truly I say to you ,To extent that you did not do it to one of these least ones, you did not do it to me"* (New World Translation Bible,1984). The time of selfishness has passed and watching out for the least should be the main focus.

Conclusion

We are in a moment of transition. It's up to us to bring back the notion of *shared responsibility* or continue to use the *blame game* to justify our need for power and greed. For our future's sake, I hope we make the right decision.

October 17th

For What It's Worth: Volume 2

The last 4 years showed the world that our collective financial house wasn't in order. The U.S and Great Britain and a few other countries are making strides but we only have to look at Greece, Spain and Portugal to see how the world market is affected by these countries mishandling of their finances. The people of these affected countries know that they're losing their pensions, their jobs and their way of life.

For the citizens of these affected countries life is over as they know it. The long vacations, the great pension plan, and the exceptional benefit packages are gone. The likely model that these countries will follow is that of the U.S. The eight hour work week; the two day weekend; the two week sick leave; the two week vacation; the 401K plan instead of a pension; this is what the future holds for you because the politicos couldn't keep their hand out the cookie jar and made bad investments.

October 24th

Review of the Last Presidential Debate

1lovejoy nation, I witnessed a good ole' ass whipping given by **President Obama** to **Mitt Romney** in the last **Presidential Debate**. Most critics and pundits gave the first debate to Mr. Romney and the second to the President. This last debate was for all the marbles; the last chance that both men had to make a lasting impression on the voting public.

Mitt Romney's Performance

The topic was **Foreign policy** and Mr. Romney had no idea what the heck he was talking about. He was inept, naive and just plain uninformed about what's going on in our changing world. Someone from his staff should have been fired that very evening for making him look so dumb.

Mr. Romney seemed to agree with the President on his foreign policy agenda. However, on the campaign trail, Mr. Romney went against all the foreign policy decisions the President made, but now he agrees? What? I guess if your only foreign policy is to increase the size of the Navy then the world is in trouble.

President Obama's Performance

President Obama's approach to this debate was the same as the second debate- measured, assertive and pressing Mr. Romney on the issues. When Mr. Romney tried to bring the issues back to domestic affairs- the President engaged with him and brought the issues right back to foreign policy. Foreign policy is the President's domain and he owned it. You could see Mr. Romney's face turning red because he knew he was in trouble and wished for this debate to end quickly.

And the Winner Is...

It was clear as day that the President won the debate. As stated before, Mr. Romney was out of his element. The President said it best about Mr. Romney's foreign policy stand (paraphrasing), *"Mr. Romney you have to be clear on where you stand and it appears you stand for nothing."* I've couldn't have said it better.

November 7th

Common Sense Prevails

Every once in a while the human race uses their common sense. Every once in a while the good guy wins. Every once in a while man can sleep a little better at night knowing that he/she did the right thing. That's what happened with the re-election of President Obama.

The forces on the other side try to paint a picture that the world was doomed under the President's leadership. However, the people know that this man is measured, intelligent and is looking out for the common man because he can relate to the struggle of everyday life. The President used his life experience and applied it to governing the people he serves. That's true leadership.

There is more work to get America and the world back to a place where peace, understanding and financial security is achievable. America voted for the President because he has a proven track record of getting things done. It may take a while but he always comes through.

America knew what type of leader they had in President Obama. Why change course when we are so close to cleaning up the follies and mishaps of the previous Bush 43rd administration. This was a long race but at the end-common sense prevails and the world is a better place knowing that American's made the right choice.

November 14th

Mitt Hearts G.O.P

When Republican Presidential nominee Mitt Romney began his quest for the Presidency of the United States, he never dreamt that he and his party would lose the election in such a big way. The American people sent a clear message to Mr. Romney and the Republican Party that their tomfoolery and obstructionist government has to stop and that common sense and civility should be the order of the day.

In the aftermath of the election, I was thinking, if Mr. Romney had written a letter to Republican Party supporters- it would go a little something like this:

Greetings 53%'ers,

> *It was a privilege to run as your party candidate for the Presidency. Despite our best efforts we did not win. I just don't understand how we lost this election? All the polling indicated that white males prefer us over Mr. Obama and his party. Our*

polling for the wealthiest Americans and right-wing religious extremist had us ahead as well.

We had a full proof strategy that was hard to beat- create voter's I.D. laws, use race and religious baiting, stop immigration reforms, suppress the right to form unions, privatize health care, disregard minorities/women and sexual equality rights, ignore young voters and support the buildup of the military industrial complex. All these strategies worked for Ronald Reagan- I wonder why it didn't work for us this time? The mainstream media is saying that the face of America is changing. I don't know what America they're living in- all I know is the America I love is white, wealthy and free.

As I write this letter from my villa in Switzerland, I will forever be grateful to all the CEO's and Super-Pac's that funded my campaign. I only wish that I could repay you back with a cabinet appointment, tax breaks and big government contracts. It just wasn't enough time to sucker those 47%'ers- it just wasn't enough time. At the end you don't have to worry about me- I have millions in the bank.

Forever Yours,

Mitt

p.s. I'll be seeing all of you at the private country clubs soon.

November 21st

Giving Thanks: Volume 2

In the United States- Thanksgiving is the official start of the holiday season. It's also a time for families to come together and get reacquainted with one another. On this holiday- we are to reflect on the many blessings that were bestowed on us this year. This blog will make a conscience effort every year to present a list of what the *1Lovejoy* blog is thankful for. Without further ado –here's the list.

I'm thankful that President Obama was re-elected
I'm thankful that the *'Tea Party'* is almost destroyed
I'm thankful that Mitt Romney is not President
I'm thankful that conservatives and Republicans are confused about how they lost the election
I'm thankful that the 2012 political/election cycle is over with
I'm thankful that justice is being pursued in the *phone-hacking scandal*
I'm thankful that the world is in a *transitional phase*
I'm thankful to those loyal readers who follow this blog
I'm thankful for Japan and the city of New Orleans
I'm thankful that the war in Afghanistan will soon come to an end
I'm thankful for my partner and the way that she loves me
I'm thankful for my family
I'm thankful to live in the greatest country in the world
I'm thankful for shelter, food in my stomach and a bed to rest my head
I'm thankful for libations-especially an ice cold Vodka Martini
I'm thankful to the people I met
I'm thankful for the advice I was given
I'm thankful for the wisdom I've gained

December 12ᵗʰ

A Family Affair

During the holiday season, people will travel far and wide to visit family. Some people do this to catch-up and re-connect with loved ones and to reminisce on days of yester years. Other people feel obligated to spend time with family because they have no choice and because it's a tradition that is a yearly occurrence.

For the people who fit into the latter category a word of advice- it's only for a little while. You may not ever see certain members of your family again. They may fall into some dire circumstance that will be their peril. Cherish the moments you share with them- good or bad; happy or sad.

Remember it's not as bad as it seems. And if you disagree with this notice- then you should have some adult egg nog or libations to ease into the transition of tolerating your loved ones.

2013

"People are trapped by history and history is trapped in them."

— James A. Baldwin

January 2nd

Respect

With a number of unfortunate events that ended the year - 2013 gives each of us an opportunity to start anew. The word "*Respect*" should be on our collective hearts, minds and tongues in this New Year. Last year, it seemed that everyone was invading everyone's comfort zone and showed a level of disrespect to their fellow man/woman. We, as human beings must make an effort to respect each other and treat each other as we would like to be treated. I hope we can do this- can we?

January 16th

Good Riddance...112th Congress

In the brief history of the United States, there has been some bad Congress but never as awful as the 112th Congress. They will forever be known as the "*Tea Party*" Congress. This particular Congress was made up of people with neo-conservative points of view whose main purpose was to derail the presidency of Mr. Obama. The result was a backlash of public support for the President and huge losses in the House of Representatives which saw surprising gains for Democrats. This was a doomed strategy from the start and their collective brain trust and conservative think tanks led them to their Waterloo.

The Problem

The neo- conservative voices underestimated the President's popularity and mistook general debate about his policies as a general disliking of the President. Their demeanor came across as bitter old white men that appeared to be bulling the President every step of the way. Also, their talk of protecting the wealthy and cutting benefits and aid for the elderly and the poor in the midst of a worldwide global recession wasn't the best message to send to the public at large.

Moreover, their constant tomfoolery over the *federal budget*, raising the *debt ceiling* and the *"fiscal cliff"* fiasco showed that they were willing to collapse the economy to protect the wealthy and big corporations. When the economy needed all hands on deck they were willing to protect the few and not the many.

Conclusion

I hope the new 113th Congress will be better than their predecessors. I hope they do the people's work, and not fall into the trap of a 'K' Street lobbyist who promises to finance their next election if they vote to keep the tax rate low for corporations and the wealthy. Let's hope that they believe in pragmatism and cooperation to solve the pressing issues that our country and world deserves. Like it or not we are now a global community and the decisions made by these people affects us all. It's time to stop thinking locally and start thinking globally.

January 23rd

The Way Forward

President Obama's inauguration speech was basically domestically driven. His speech reminded me of the 16th President's second inauguration speech- Abraham Lincoln. Just like Mr. Lincoln – Mr. Obama tried to evoke the spirit of unity that if one of us falls behind then we all fail. Moreover, a sense of purpose to do the will of the people was evident in both speeches as well.

The Tone

The tone in their speeches seemed to be of men who've been driven to their knees only to rise up and start anew to fight for those who can't fight for themselves. In both speeches, they seemed to be wary of petty arguments and petty leaders unwilling to make the difficult decisions that need to be made to ensure the common good. In both speeches, these men are willing to do the right thing for everyone and just not the privileged few.

A Look Ahead

Just like Mr. Lincoln- Mr. Obama looks a little bit older, a little bit greyer and appears to be a little wiser. Again, just like Mr. Lincoln- Mr. Obama is an intelligent man and now knows the perils that await him. It will serve Mr. Obama well to learn from the 16th President because he gave a road map on how to be a great man and a great President. Godspeed, Mr. Obama.

The Importance of Black History Month

With the advent of President Barack Obama becoming the first African-American to serve as Commander-In–Chief, some critics say that *Black History Month* is a thing of the past and is no longer needed. To those critics I say that there's still a need for this particular celebration now more than ever. In this commentary I hope to illuminate why Black History Month is still an important observance.

Origins

In 1926, historian Dr. Carter G. Woodson created *"Negro History Week"* to fall on the second week of February to honor President Abraham Lincoln and Frederick Douglas' birthdays. Dr. Woodson hoped that this celebration would showcase the accomplishments and contributions of Blacks in America when the country was in the midst of apartheid. The creation of this celebration was embraced by the black community and progressive whites alike. As popularity of the celebration grew most mayors embraced the week as well. In 1976, the federal government extended the week into a month by acknowledging the efforts of Kent State's Black Student leaders who were doing so since 1970.

Importance

The importance of Black History Month is as important now than ever before. Many white Americans are in denial of the mistreatment of African Americans throughout the history of America- even to this day. Kidnapping of a people from their native lands; the triangle slave trade; slave labor; human degradation, segregation, lynching's, housing discrimination, breaking the color- barriers in sports, civil rights movement, voting rights, poor housing and schools in majority black neighborhoods, police brutality, Hurricane Katrina, lack of employment opportunities are reminders of why some critics are wrong to want to do away with this celebration. Despite all the trials and tribulations they rose up and became productive members of society and overcame the odds stacked against them.

Conclusion

African- Americans are the soul of America. The contributions made by countless talented people of color cannot be ignored. The reason Black History Month should continue is to remind us that African- Americans are a strong and proud people. America should be reminded of it's disgusting past. America should be reminded that the promises made are still unfulfilled. America should be proud of the progress but it needs to strive for more.

February 27th

The Blame Game

With the upcoming sequester looming on March 1st the federal government funding will basically be cut in half. This is not the first time that the U.S. economy is held hostage nor will it be the last. We can blame the neo-conservatives in Congress for creating this mess or we can place blame where it should belong- with Grover Norquist.

Background

Grover Norquist is a Harvard educated conservative libertarian who is the founder and president of the organization - *Americans for Tax Reform*. This organization managed to get neo-conservative Republicans in Congress sign a pledge not to raise taxes under any circumstance. Mr. Norquist's organization held neo- conservative's feet to the fire and threatened those who reconsidered. Mr. Norquist was on a one man mission to bring down the economy of the United States and defeat President Obama in the process. Both plans backfired- Mr. Obama is still President of the United States and the economy is on the rise.

Conclusion

With the upcoming sequester and two more years of Republicans creating budget battles- we have one man to thank- Grover Norquist. It's amazing how a man who did not run for political office, nor held any position in public life can wheel the power of a political boss. The election is over and the Republican Party needs to tell people of Mr. Norquist's ilk to just go away. The Republicans in Congress need to put the people first and not be tied to some ideological fool who isn't beholden to anyone. In other words- do your job. The last two years were an all-out effort to derail Mr. Obama's presidency- it didn't happen. Now it's time to stop this tomfoolery and do the work of the people; because if you don't you'll be working for Mr. Norquist and wondering why you were beholden to this ivy league, neo-conservative intellectual quack who doesn't live in the real world. Like most people in academia he thinks in theories which do not apply to real world applications.

March 13ᵗʰ

The Mental Health Issue

Once again recent gun violence in the U.S. has triggered the debate on gun control. A growing number of people are raising the issue of mental health as the cause of these recent tragedies. It's true that these now infamous figures that were able to obtain these weapons were mentally disturbed, but there's a deeper issue at hand- the lack of funding for mental health facilities. This issue goes back to Ronald Reagan's administration and this commentary will explain when political philosophy can have dire consequences a generation later.

Reagan's War on Mental Health

In the 1980's, the Reagan administration went on the war path to cut programs that would benefit the elderly and the poor in our society. His administration cut these programs to build up the military industrial complex. The thinking was to outspend the former Soviet Union on weapons and in effect crumple their economy - it worked. However, trickle- down economics and the biggest deficit in American history sent the U.S. economy crashing in 1987 when the stock market took a nose drive. It took 2 years for the U.S. economy to recover.

The agenda was an all-out effort to destroy the Soviet Union, carry favor with the military and cater to the wealthy. The Reagan administration forgot about the needs of most Americans- especially those with mental health issues. At the same time, funding for state hospitals was eliminated and research for studying this disease was at a snail's pace. Mental health hospitals were replaced with privately owned prisons that needed bodies to fill up their facilities to justify funding. This system is still in place.

The Reagan administration was focused on funding a secret war (Iran-Contra Scandal), Culture Wars, and the rise of the Moral Majority. The notion of looking out for your fellow American was a thing of the past. The heroes of the civil rights era were gone and were replaced by characters like *Gordon Gekko* (played by Michael Douglas) depicted in the movie *"Wall Street"*. In the 80's –the mantra became *"Greed is good."*

Legacy

If you visit places like San Francisco's Civic Center; Los Angeles' Skid Row; Anchorage's downtown, you will see the vivid reality of homelessness and mental illness. The justice system needs to stop locking up people with mental disabilities in privately owned prisons- this is not the solution. Reopening state mental institutions to study the effect of mental illness is the correct solution to what we are seeing now. With these tragic incidents we have an opportunity to diagnose and to move forward with a solution.

And if you still don't think this problem affects you, ask Congresswoman Gabrielle Giffords; the town of Aurora, Colorado and the town of Newtown, Connecticut. The time to act is now!

Homeless man on a San Francisco street

Rupert Murdoch's Phone-Hacking Scandal- What's Happened?

Rupert Murdoch's entertainment division of *News Corp* announced that it will form a new 24 hour sports channel to rival *ESPN*. Murdoch is confident about this venture because he challenged the 24 hour news channel *CNN* by developing Fox News - a conservative alternative to his rival. Fast forward to the present and Fox News is consistently leading the ratings of 24 hours cable news. This venture is the latest expansion of the Murdoch Empire. However, there are still unanswered questions about the *bribery of foreign officials* and the ongoing saga of the *phone-hacking scandal*. These issues are bellowing underneath the surface and need to be judged before any expansion of this man's empire continues.

Bribery

Since the revelation of the phone-hacking scandal was brought to light by the late journalist *Sean Hoare* - there is a plethora of evidence exposing the corruption that was ever present at News Corp. Since News Corp is an American Corporation, it's illegal for it to engage in any sort of bribery of any foreign official(s) under any circumstance. The phone-hacking scandal exposed bribery at every conceivable level.

Call for Action

Since Mr. Murdoch is a naturalized U.S. citizen and his corporation is located in the U.S. - a full Senate investigation/hearing should take place before Mr. Rupert expands his brand. It is the duty of the U.S. Senate to investigate any U.S. business involved in bribery charges overseas. This hearing is long overdue. The evidence has been complied by the British government in just a little less than two years. During that time, 2 of Mr. Murdoch's loyal lieutenants are in jail (Andy Coulson & Rebekah Brooks) and a little girl's death was exploited to sell newspapers. The American people deserve a serious investigation before any expansion of Mr. Murdoch's business ventures can take place. If his company was so cavalier in the phone-hacking scandal in Britain, imagine what he would do to bring down his competitors in the U.S.?

March 27th

The Trouble with Donations and NPO's

Recently, victims and survivors of mass shootings in the United States are coming together to provide victims of future tragic events greater control of donations being raised on their behalf. This is a move to stop nonprofit groups from holding on to donations intended for the victim's families. A group representing the families of the tragedies in Virginia Tech, Columbine and Aurora want to spare the victims of the Newtown shootings from red tape, paperwork and NPO bureaucracy. The group would like to set up a National Compassion Fund that oversees and manages future donations.

What's the Next Move?

This informal group has made contact with a senior White House official and 2 members of Congress to talk about establishing a national fund raising operation for future tragedies. The group doesn't want to name which officials they are talking to because they don't want to jeopardize the progress being made.

The Final Step

This issue was bound to come up sooner or later. The fact that this informal group is exposing nonprofit bureaucratic red tape in the light of many horrific tragedies highlights one of the reasons people don't give to nonprofits. Many people questioned if the money being raised by these nonprofit groups is truly going to the victims? With the formation of this group we have our answer. Washington D.C. attorney Kenneth Feinberg who oversaw the distributions of funds to the September 11th victim fund and the BP Oil Spill victim fund said it best, *"I think it's a great idea. The question is: Is there a political will to do it?"*

Like Father, Like Son

With the death of Kim Jong- Il, the world had high hopes for his son Kim Jong-Un. The hope was that this young leader of North Korea could finally start an open dialogue with the world powers to restore enduring peace and economic stability to the Korean peninsula. However, the world is finding out that the son is far worse than his father. With his recent rhetoric of war and nuclear destruction the world doesn't know whether to take his threats seriously or not.

Absolute Power

It appears since Kim Jong-Un is an unproven leader he wants to show the world that he is not to be trifled with. He wants to show his people that he is not afraid of the West (namely the United States) and he won't become a puppet of the Chinese government. He wants to be just like his father in every way- feared.

There are reports circulating around the intelligence community stating that the 7 generals who were pallbearers at his father's funeral met some ill fate; 4 out of the 7 generals just disappeared without a trace; one of the generals was made to wear a suicide vest strapped with explosives and was blown up in front of his contemporaries. If these reports are true- then we're dealing with someone who is blood thirsty for power.

The Reality

In reality, no one knows what this leader from North Korea will do. It appears that he's following the same playbook that his father has been using for years - nuclear weapons are their only bargaining chip and they know it. This recent talk of war is giving the United States and China an opportunity to engage diplomatically and give them a common purpose. I don't think Kim Jong-Un or his advisors really thought this through.

I pray that this young man will back off his rhetoric of war. I pray that his common sense will kick in. I pray that he realizes that his people are not up for a war because they are fragile from a lack of food. I pray that he sees that this is a "no- win situation". I pray he realizes that he is not his father. I pray that he realizes he can become greater that his father if he provides his people with economic stability and lasting peace in the Korean peninsula. I pray.

April 17th

Senseless

On April 15th, two bombs exploded near the finish line of the prestigious *Boston Marathon*. 176 people were injured and 3 people are dead. An 8-year-old boy was one of the victims that expired that day. President Obama addressed the American people to stay calm and not to rush to judgment until all evidence was collected and an investigation into this tragedy was concluded.

The Reality

In the back of every American's mind we knew this day would come. Threats ranging from the *"Underwear Bomber"* attempted attack in 2009, to the attempted *"Car Bomb"* attack in New York City Time Square in 2010. It seems soft targets were being tested and for the most part law enforcement officials were trained and ready for that possibility. However, with all the precaution that law enforcement take you can't prepare for everything. Whatever person or group that did this waited for their opportunity and took it.

Cowardly Act

When a person or non- state actors decide to blow up innocent people to make a statement or a political point- they are cowards. Most of the people who are caught up in these attacks are normal everyday people who are either enjoying the day with their loved ones or just making their way home. It's just their misfortune to run into some menace who wants to make some point about how disillusioned he/she is with their or somebody else's government. To all those scum out there- who is satisfied with their government? If everybody felt like these idiots there will be nothing left to blow up.

If these so called freedom fighters want to make a change just follow the example of *Dr. Martin Luther King Jr.* and *Mahatma Gandhi*. These brave men showed that one can have dignity and still change their government and the world, without acting in a violent way. Their actions spoke louder than words and that is why they are legends.

Conclusion

If it's a foreign non- state actor the weight of the United States government will crush the countries that are harboring that person or group. If it's homegrown terrorism- there will be no place to run or hide. In the history of these attacks on the United States- no one has gotten away with these actions. Ever!!!

Quincy Market. Boston MA

Skyfall

Just when things were beginning to get back to normal in the U.S. - it happened. Just after achieving some economic stability in the wake of a financial collapse that lead to a worldwide recession- it happened. Just after a bitter Presidential election- it happened. Just when the U.S. military is about to leave the Middle East Theater after disbanding a majority of al-Qaeda- it happened. Homegrown terrorism happened- with no real rhyme or reason.

The Reality

It's obvious what happened in this situation. One brother was frustrated that his life in the U.S. wasn't going according to plan so he influenced his younger sibling (who was assimilated in the U.S.) that Islam was being attacked and that they must take up the jihadist struggle to begin *Armageddon.* That's the story- plain and simple.

Fantasy of Grandeur

This blogger refuses to name the brothers because I do not want to give them any more notoriety than they already have. This is the story of family and how an older brother, wasn't his brother's keeper. I'm just sad that he involved his younger brother in his twisted fantasy of grandeur.

The Stigma

The brother's uncle said it best about the actions of his nephew's, 'They *have cursed our family's name and the Chechen people"*. For better or for worse, the Chechen people and their families will bear the burden for their senseless actions for decades to come.

Comfortable In His Own Skin

Veteran NBA player Jason Collins' recent revelation that he's gay is the first time that an active player in one of the major North America sports organizations came out of the closet. This small step marks the beginning of a new chapter in the American lexicon. It was fitting that a veteran player – on the wrong side of 30 and in the twilight of his 12 year career would be so brave to expose his life at this time. He knew that he has a few good years to give to a franchise and wants to maximize his talent and enjoy the game that he loves. He knows that because of his age and declining skills he wants to be honest in every aspect of his life, on and off the court.

Being the First

Some people in the news media and in the LGBT community wanted a male pro athlete to come out of the closet for years. This notion was totally selfish and unfair. They wanted to ask young men who averaged 21- 24 years of age to come out the closet? Please!! When people are younger they don't know what they want and Mr. Collins is not the same person that he was at 24. People change, and the older one gets the more comfortable they get in their skin and Mr. Collins is finally comfortable in his own skin.

In His Own Words

Mr. Collins didn't want to be the first pro male active player to come out of the closet. He knew that the time was right and that he already had a productive pro career. Mr. Collins said it best about his journey by saying, *"No one wants to live in fear. I've always been scared of saying the wrong thing. I don't sleep well. I never have. But each time I tell another person, I feel stronger and sleep a little more soundly. It takes an enormous amount of energy to guard such a big secret. I've endured years of misery and gone to enormous lengths to live a lie. I was certain that my world would fall apart if anyone knew. And yet when I acknowledged my sexuality I felt whole for the first time. I still had the same sense of humor, I still had the same mannerisms and my friends still had my back".*

We hope that you finally sleep well tonight Mr. Collins.

June 5th

Advice for the Class of 2013

Dear Class of 2013, you have a decision to make - be bold or follow the herd. Yes, you can maintain the status quo and follow the course your family and friends imagine for you. Or you can live your own dream and try to live the life you'd imagine for yourself. This is the most important decision that you will make in your life. It could alter your entire existence. This is the fork in your road.

In this life, many people do what they have to do to provide for themselves or their family with food, shelter and sometimes life's little indulgences. However, some people are meant to break out of that mold and truly do what they love and damn the consequences. For these people, if they don't try to achieve their dreams then they're dead already.

If you speak to someone in your family you will find someone that you know that broke out of the mold they were told they had to follow. Some of them may have failed and some may have had succeeded in the pursuit of their happiness. Regardless, if they succeeded or failed- they at least gave it a shot.

The beauty of this life is to keep picking yourself up when things are at their worst. If you can do that, in whatever endeavor you may venture, you will find your character. The poet Robert Frost wrote about 2 roads; one that was traveled frequently the other that was not. The question was raised about which road the character would travel on? However, the real question is, which road will you take? Whatever your decision- make an effort to go all out and never look back.

June 19th

Spy Games

Recently, a fellow by the name of Edward Snowden, the former National Security Agency (NSA) contractor, exposed the U.S. government's secret surveillance program. This revelation shouldn't have been a surprise to any of us but I'm outraged at the response this news has received from mass media at large. Like it or not-the U.S. is still at war and people of Edward Snowden's ilk make it that much more difficult to stop non-state actors from doing harm to the average Mr. & Mrs. John Q. Public. We're not fighting countries anymore- we're in constant battles with people that have extreme points of views or wanting world domination and control. We have only to re-examine the last few months to see what I mean (i.e. Boston Marathon Bombers & the London Knife Attack).

The Reality

The reality is that the average American (or person for that matter) wants to feel safe and protected in their community; have shelter; food in their bellies; a pillow to lay their head on and the right to pursue their ambition. Those rights were put to the test when the U.S. Congress passed *"The Patriot Act"* after the attacks of 9/11. Every American knew that this new law would allow the U.S. President full range to hunt down anyone who was connected with the attacks on 9/11. We all knew this. Now that we see the end of war in sight - we are upset that our information is being looked at. This is hypocrisy at its best. People give more information to organizations like Google and Facebook- than to the U.S. government.

In Conclusion

I'm not defending the actions of the government but you have to be naïve to believe that government isn't monitoring its citizens. And for your part- you're a willing participant in your surveillance; i.e. passport, computers, cell phones and any other electronic device available. If you have nothing to hide then this issue shouldn't bother you. However, if you're keeping some secret from your loved ones- then you may have a problem with this whole thing.

Freedom, it's free. And for the countless men and women who safeguard us from harm- they shouldn't be a criticized for doing their jobs. When the war in Afghanistan is over, I will think a little differently about this issue. But don't think for a moment that there won't be someone hearing and watching our every move- that's of course if you're doing something wrong.

July 10th

How to Stop a Dictator from Becoming a Dictator

If you had a chance to kill Adolph Hitler and to save 6 million people from genocide and prevent a World War- what will you do? This question is brought up in countless movies, television shows, books and general discussions. A rational person would say "yes" to the killing of this agent of evil to save countless families from the heartache of war. In a modern day parallel, we can look at Egypt and how the people removed their first democratically elected President- Mohamed Morsi and his political party The Muslim Brotherhood from power. The Egyptian people read the writing on the wall and put a stop to Mr. Morsi's thirst for power.

A Coup or Not a Coup...

Most mass media outlets in the West were quick to say that if someone's elected democratically by the people and who is forcibly remove from office is caught up in a Coup d'état. In theory, that is true, but the people in Egypt saw a man who was elected to office because he promised to bring all Egyptians' together.

Instead, Mr. Morsi attempted to consolidate power to his political organization; tried to arrest people who made fun of him or his government; neglected the country's poor infrastructure; failed to address a weak economy; allowed the rise of religious intolerants; tolerated a spike in the number of gang rapes/rapes and dissolved the constitution to enact a new constitution that favors Islamic beliefs. This all took place within a year.

Prevention

The reason for the Arab Spring was to bring down dictators in the Arab world who didn't provide for the people. The Egyptian people saw that Mr. Morsi didn't provide for his people and would use his political party to rule with an iron fist for years to come; taking money from Western powers while at the same time condemning them to play up to his political base. I think we've seen this before.

In closing, this blogger praises the Egyptian people for putting a stop to this power hungry leader. In a democracy – all must be represented and provided for and not just the privileged few.

July 17th

The End of Racism: Volume 2

In the U.S. there continues to be nationwide protest in major cities over the acquittal of George Zimmerman in the second degree murder case of 17 year old teenager Trayvon Martin. We have yet to hear from any jurors provide a reasonable explanation regarding the decision to acquit the volunteer neighborhood watchman who got out of his car to follow Mr. Martin; provoked him without just cause; then grabbed and shot him in the chest at close range.

The Trend

This verdict has rekindled the debate about race and civil rights in the U.S. A number of laws that are said to protect citizens harkens back to"Jim Crow" era. Here are a few examples:

(1) "Stop and Frisk" - In New York City this law gives police officers the right to stop anyone at any time but African- American & Latino males are disproportionately targeted.

(2) 24 states passed laws that are equal to the *"Stand Your Ground"* law that Mr. Zimmerman used in his defense. The *"Stand Your Ground"* law simply states that if you feel threatened then you have the right to use deadly force to protect yourself.

(3) Section 4 is the Supreme Court's recent decision to deem the Voting Right Act unconstitutional. This decision rips at the heart of a law which protects minorities (mainly in the South) right to vote. Unfortunately, there are more glaring examples of how minorities feel disrespected by the system.

If there's a silver-lining to these absurd events is that African –Americans (minorities in general) finally feel confident that these incidents won't go unnoticed. With the President's bully pulpit and Attorney General Eric Holder standing watch, the community as a whole can take comfort that someone who looks like them will look out for their best interest. This is a different feeling than the hopelessness that civil right activists have felt in years pass.

The Reality

America you need to wake up. If we claim to be a nation of laws then we should live by those principles. If you don't like someone because the way they look, act, or dress- that's your problem. If you take the time to talk to people different from yourself you might be surprised how similar you are. This notion of a pastime paradise is absurd. If you live in the past then you are letting the future pass you by. America- united we stand- divided we fall. Wake Up!!

July 31st

Here We Go Again: The Looming Budget Battle

In the summertime, the members of Congress usually take a hiatus from Washington D.C. to hear from their constituents and financial sponsors about the issues that concern them. Then in September, they return, ready to work hard and pass meaningful legislation for the betterment of their fellow countryman. There was a time when this was true- now members of Congress take their marching orders from financial sponsors and political pundits to score points, to carry favor with their respective party leaders and to advance their cache' for more power. This is the harsh reality of the political landscape today.

When Congress comes back in September, the federal budget will be back on the table once again. President Obama wants to break this stalemate by reintroducing the *"Grand Bargain"*. This proposal, essentially lowers the tax rates for corporations (from 35% to 28%) and invests in community college education along with public work projects. This proposal is a compromise that gives the Republicans the tax breaks they want for corporations while stimulating the economy which the Democrats want. Everyone has skin in the game and everyone gets what they want-right? However, the Republicans are quick to dismiss the proposal saying that this is another round of stimulus.

With the 2014 mid-term elections on the horizon, the Republican Party are playing a game of chicken, trying to cater to their conservative base to stand up to President Obama, hoping that he will crave in to their demands for reinstating the Bush tax cuts for the wealthy. The Federal Reserve Board, Wall Street experts and credit agencies are urging the Republican-controlled House of Representatives that if another budget battle ensues that the economy will head for another recession.

President Obama is trying to make the case to the American people that compromise is the key to solve this pressing issue and for the country to move forward together. The Republican Party is holding steadfast to their ideology and conservative principles; the same principles which lost them seats in the 2012 election cycle. I think House Speaker John Boehner needs to crack the whip and get these idiots in line, accept the compromise and move on. A year is too long to drag this issue out. By accepting the compromise everyone saves face and the financial markets will be happy. Please spare the American people (and the world) the fiasco that was the last budget battle. Remember, compromise equals common sense.

August 7th

Farewell Letter to Mahmoud Ahmadinejad

Dear Mahmoud,

These last eight years with you as Iran's President has been simply- awful. The multitudes of problems that your country has is unthinkable in a so-called modern society - an heroin epidemic; high HIV rates; high unemployment rates; extreme poverty; poor quality of life; religious extremism- and that's not even the worst part of your presidency.

You have managed to ignore recent history and pronounced to the world that the Jewish Holocaust was a fabrication. Moreover, you threaten the state of Israel with total destruction knowing that the United States is an ally of the Jewish State.

Then your country engaged in uranium enrichment; which is clearly to produce nuclear weapons but you stated time and again that it is strictly for peaceful purposes. I'm just glad that you had no say or power over that program or we'd all be in a nuclear winter.

Mahmoud, because of your constant tomfoolery and your unwillingness to engage in meaningful dialogue, you have caused heartache and financial ruin for your country in the form of sanctions. Now your country is reduced to bartering with other countries just to get the basic necessities.

Mr. Ahmadinejad, you have brought more problems to your country then solutions. I'm sure that the Supreme Leader Hassan Rouhani; Iran; the Middle East Region and the rest of the world will not miss your antics anytime soon. Good riddance.

Regards,

The World

Stop and Frisk: Ruled Unconstitutional

This blog posting will be short and sweet. I will not go into the history of the *Stop- and- Frisk* policy because I have written about this unjust law on several occasions. This policy targeted so-called high crime areas and minority neighborhoods. On Monday, a federal judge ruled that in New York City, the procedure of *stop- and- frisk* is unconstitutional under federal law because an individual's civil rights are violated under this policy. This ruling should be celebrated because this policy harkened back to the *"Jim Crow"* era. Now, if a police officer wants to *stop-and-frisk* someone (namely minorities), they have to have '*just cause*'. This is the common sense approach that should have been implemented in the first place. With this ruling- common sense prevails.

September 4th

A Savvy Political Stroke

The Syrian government has led a chemical attack upon their civilian population in an effort to quell the civil war. President Obama along with the leaders of Great Britain and France wanted to put an end to the potential spread of chemical weapons before it can be used on western powers and their allies- namely Israel. Last week the British Parliament rejected a military option to stop the Syrian government from using these weapons. The cry for the rejection was the hard lessons from the Iraq War; the slogan, "heed *the war in Iraq*".

Now that the British Parliament has rejected the military option, President Obama could easily have bombed the chemical facilities and crumpled the Syrian military to make a point that this type of behavior is unacceptable. However, President Obama is taking a different route- he is calling on the U.S. Congress to grant him permission to strike Syria. He is doing this because (1) he wants to get a record of each member of Congress who are in favor for/against this action; (2) to stop any talk of impeachment and (3) to cause infighting within the Republican Party.

On the Record

Each member of Congress loves to go on these political talk shows to share their insight on the hot political issues of the day. The flip-flopping of their opinions are always amazing and sad at the same time. In this case, President Obama wants to hold their feet to the fire and make them take a stand. Most of these Politician's love taking about how the U.S. needs to protect the state of Israel from any sort of attack- now it's their time to put up or shut up.

Talk of Impeachment

For weeks the Republican Party was rumored to be dreaming up some scenario that they can bring President Obama up on impeachment charges. Their first avenue was the new *Affordable Healthcare Act* (Obamacare) but the Supreme Court upheld that the new law did not violate the U.S. Constitution. However, the *War Power Act* would have given them the perfect opportunity to make this into a political issue in the upcoming 2014 mid-term elections. Even though the President has the right under the law to use this power to protect the interest of the United States. Don't forget that the talk of impeachment was rampant when President Obama issued the air strikes against Libya. Now, President Obama has turned the tables on the Republicans in Congress to stop the spread of chemical weapons or be forced to answer to Israeli lobbyist groups about their failure to protect their country.

Republican Infighting

This vote will be a fight to see who will win the soul of this political party the *Hawks* or the *Isolationist*. The *Hawks* believe that the United States has a moral obligation to protect the innocent around the world from evil and that military might is a clear way of showing U.S. superiority. The *Isolationist* believes that the world needs to take care of their own problems and if they got themselves into a situation then they can surely figure it out. This will be an interesting debate that will be played out for the world to see.

Many political pundits and political figures thought they knew the tendencies of President Obama but once again they were wrong. President Obama is putting up a mirror to his political friends and foes; and to the world at large saying that this is wrong and we have to do something about it. He's making the world question itself. Now that's a savvy stroke of political genius.

October 23rd

You Lost...Get Over It.

The fiasco that was the fiscal budget debate that partially shut down half of the U.S. government service for over a 16 day period - due in part because Tea Party Republicans wanted to gut out or delay the new Affordable Health Care Law (Obamacare) - is finally over. This move cost the U.S. government over 23 Billion dollars, caused worldwide markets to panic and created a growing mistrust of the political system. However, the same people who brought this self-inflicted wound to the public are still vowing to fight. Even arch conservatives like Grover Norquist and Senator Mitch McConnell (R-Kentucky) are calling for an end of this tomfoolery method. It didn't work in 1995 and it hasn't worked now.

When the government shutdown both times, the Republican Party was the culprit. The so-called party for the wealthy and the business community were willing to stop commerce to satisfy their benefactors who fund their campaigns and who will become their future employer when their days in Congress are over. This foolish move only strengthened the idea that Republicans can't do their jobs. It's like the Republican Party is running a never-ending campaign to cater to their gerrymander voting block and to test the waters of the national spotlight. This latest version of arch-conservatism is extreme and dangerous to the worldwide economy.

Fortunately, the American people can send a message to Congress that this tomfoolery is no longer acceptable. With the 2014 election cycle upon us- I urge reasonable people to campaign against these people who call themselves "Tea Party" conservatives. The movement was politically entertaining for a while but it's now gotten to a point that these people have no business in government. Enough is enough! If the only platform that you had to run on was defeating President Obama in the 2012 election and repealing The Affordable Healthcare Act- then you lost on both counts.

The American people should vote these Tea Party conservatives out of office. The government shutdown was like their Custer's Last Stand. And I'm hoping just like Custer- this movement will meet a bloody end.

November 6th

Seems Like Old Times: Volume 2

Once again, 2 incidents of gun violence in the U.S. have reared its ugly head. I could go on about the need to place greater restrictions on people who would purchase guns, but I won't. I could go on to advocate that the gun shows needs to be eliminated from the American landscape, but I won't. I could go on about the need to focus attention on the mentally ill and the issues they face, but I won't.

The powers that be are making far too much money on the gun culture that has been established in the United States for decades. Notable groups like the powerful National Rifle Association (NRA) cater and lobby for gun manufacture's interest. They will fight any law that interrupts the flow of business, claiming that they're protecting U.S. citizens 2nd amendment rights granted under the U.S. Constitution. This my friends, is bullshit.

If the latest incidents in New Jersey and Los Angeles haven't changed your mind on sensible gun reform legislation, then your mind will never be changed. With the holiday season upon us this kind of horrific tragedy will eventually happen again on a bloody scale. So go ahead and ignore common sense, gun control legislation and the mentally ill because another tragedy is inevitable.

November 20ᵗʰ

So It Begins- The Holiday Season

Next weekend will be Thanksgiving in America. This traditional celebration marks the beginning of the Christmas or Holiday season. Most of us will spend time with our families remembering the days of yester years. However, if you want to get through Thanksgiving without killing one of your relatives – here's a few tips to get you through this time of the year.

1. **Always have a libation nearby**- Remember, you always want a drink in your hand because if someone asks you an idiotic question or makes a sly remark- you can always sip a tasty libation to forget the insult(s) and ignore them for the rest of your time there.
2. **Make sure you watch football**- All day long, football will be playing. This is a refuge from the chaotic atmosphere around you. Why do you think your father and uncle watch these games every Thanksgiving? Sit, watch and learn from the masters on how to avoid your relatives.
3. **Be the person to run errands**- When there's a chance to get away from the house- take it.

I hope these little titbits are helpful in getting you through the day. Good Luck out there.

November 27ᵗʰ

Giving Thanks: Volume 3

In the United States- Thanksgiving is the official start of the holiday season. It's also a time for families to come together and get reacquainted with one another. On this holiday- we are to reflect on the many blessings that were bestowed on us this year. This blog will make a conscience effort every year to present a list of what the *1Lovejoy* blog is thankful for. Without further ado –here's the list.

I'm thankful that Keith Olbermann is back on television
I'm thankful that the Obama administration is going after Super Pacs
I'm still thankful that Mitt Romney is not President
I'm thankful that conservatives and Republicans look silly after the self-inflicted debt-ceiling episode
I'm thankful that peace talks will be held to end the Syrian civil war.
I'm thankful that justice is being pursued in the *phone-hacking scandal*
I'm thankful that the New Orleans Saints are rebounding from the so-called Bounty-gate scandal
I'm thankful to those loyal readers who follow this blog
I'm thankful for the city of New Orleans
I'm thankful that Iran is trying to curb their nuclear ambitions
I'm thankful for my partner and the way that she loves me
I'm thankful for my family
I'm thankful for shelter, food in my stomach and a pillow to rest my head
I'm thankful for libations-especially an ice cold Vodka Martini
I'm thankful for the advice I was given
I'm thankful for the wisdom I've gained

December 4th

Let Us Ponder For a Moment

Let us ponder for a moment about the things that are going on in our collective world. In the world today- a display of common courtesy is sorely lacking. A simple gesture of opening the door for someone; or helping an elderly person walk across the street are just a few example of how human beings can be civil to one other.

Instead, we isolate ourselves behind our laptops and make insulting, non-constructive comments on social media outlets to voice some pent up anger that harbors some deep, dark issues that only surface when you know that you are anonymous. This is not the way human beings are supposed to interact with each other. Please tell me this is not the way forward?

During this Holiday Season- reflect on your behavior towards your fellow human beings. Try to treat others as you would want to be treated because karma is a motherfucker.

December 11th

A Christmas Wish: Volume 2

The late great cartoonist Charles M. Schulz once said that, *"Christmas is doing a little something extra for someone."* I guess that's what the Holiday Season is all about- just showing a little bit of kindness to everyone. If we can keep to those principles of goodwill towards all mankind- what a wonderful world this could be.

1lovejoy Nation- let's make a pledge to watch out for one another just a little bit. I don't mean go out your way to show a little bit of kindness but just do what you can; like saying a kind word if someone's feeling down or buy someone a beer just because. These are random act of kindness that can make someone's day. If we can be a little understanding during this time of year- why can't we exhibit this behavior the whole year through?

2014

"Look back, and smile on perils past."

– Walter Scott

January 1

2014 Mantra: I Quit!!!

2013 was the last year of the *Great Recession*. We can see signs of improvements in the rise of consumer spending, employers hiring, the housing market and the stock market. This trend points to things returning back to normal. You can see it in our political discussion- from economic politics to the culture wars in our society. Yes, things are definitely back to normal.

When the Great Recession hit- more employers demanded more out of their employees and in some cases this involved 1 person doing the job of 3 people. If their employees didn't cater to their demands they would be fired or let go due to uncontrollable happenstance. Since the economy appears to be back on track, you will see more people quitting their thankless jobs in the pursuit for better employment.

The most popular viral videos of 2013 were that of people quitting their jobs. I believe that this trend will continue because people will find out that their employers are concerned about the bottom-line and their bonuses.

So remember, you read it here first, people will quit their shitty jobs to work in an environment where their opinion matters and where their work is valued.

February 5th

America's New Slavery System: Prison

For most people who are disenfranchised and uneducated, a gloomy scenario of poverty or incarceration is the likely road ahead. People who are in this predicament haven't the life skills to turn their situations around due to a number of trials and tribulations and can be marginalized as people that are not to be trusted. The system has failed these people.

161

Recently, The National Registry of Exonerations presented their 2013 annual report that revealed a record number of convictions (87) were overturned due to DNA evident or witness intimidation by police detectives. This report shouldn't be a surprise to most people. It shows that there is something extremely wrong with the criminal justice system in America today.

If the judicial system is where people come to find justice, then we as a nation must call for common sense reforms in the criminal justice system to protect innocent people from serving time for a crime they didn't commit. This should not happen- we're better than this.

July 30th

Let Them Have Cake: The FIFA World Cup

The 2014 FIFA World Cup was enjoyed by millions the world over. The enormous success of the game was felt especially in the United States who viewed the matches more than ever before. Sport commentators and soccer enthusiasts believe that the so-called *"Beautiful Game"* will be the next big thing in the United States. These people have been saying the same thing since the last century. Reality check- it will never happen!

The Push

In the United States, the push to popularize soccer or futbol has failed miserably. The most glaring example is when the great Brazilian soccer player Pele (1970's) and David Beckham (2000's) were promoting the world game to the American masses. It was a nice try but these guys were on the back end of their careers and were past their prime.

The Racism

As a casual observer, I've seen protests in the soccer world against racism. As a minority, my antenna was raised to the racial abuse reported by North and Sub-Sahara- African players. The most famous incident occurred during the 2006 FIFA World Cup Finals when the French Algerian player Zidane was told that his mother was a "terrorist" by an Italian player. Zidane responded with a head butt and got red carded out of the match. This kind of behavior is encouraged to "rattle an opponent". To this day, this is accepted as a "strategy". If this kind of behavior is strategy-then it's a bad one.

Better Athletes

By far, the United States have the best athletes in the world. However, our best athletes do not play soccer. The best athletes can be found playing in the NFL, NBA, NHL and MLB. The money is immediate and the perks are great. There is no real incentive in the states to play the so-called "Beautiful Game" as there is overseas in Europe or South America.

A Niche Sport

The game of soccer in the United States is quickly becoming a niche sport because the people who understand the nuances of the game view novices to the sport as ignorant hicks. I'm sorry if I get perturbed if every five minutes someone is falling to the ground giving a bad method acting performance of being injured. Again, this is what they call "strategy".

Let Them Have This Moment

Every four years in the Olympics, the United States comes either first or second in the overall medal counts. Like every American, I cheer for our young men and women to do well and make our country proud. I'm sure that every country feels that way about their athletes, but in the World Cup- they actually have a chance. As Americans we are used to winning but let the world have their moment. We are already hated for winning everything so let them have this one. Let other countries revel in this game started by Europeans that was meant for them to enjoy. Let's face it- we are the unwelcome guest.

So to my fellow Americans, let's just be happy that our boys made us proud and treat this like an Olympic event that we are never supposed to win.

August 6th

The Mayans Were Almost Right

On July 23rd 2012, according to NASA, a powerful Sun storm rampaged through Earth's orbit which nearly sent civilization back to the 18th Century.

Nearly two years to the date of this phenomenon the space agency released this information last month on their website. According to experts, anything that depends on electricity and our mobile devices would have been obsolete. I'm talking about the loss of GPS, mobile phones, laptops and even the water supply that depends on electric pumps. We, as a collective human race, would have been in a world of pain.

According to physicist Pete Riley who published a paper on this topic, *"There is a 12 percent chance of a super solar storm the size of the Carrington event hitting Earth in the next 10 years."*

Reality Check

In the last couple of years, I wrote about the doomsday scenarios of the late Harold Camping and the tomfoolery made of the Mayans 2012 prediction. But to actually read scientific evidence is mind blowing. It's just a bit odd that this information was released to the public 2 years after the fact. One wonders, why didn't the scientific community inform the public? Did the powers that be have anything to do with stopping this information getting out to the masses until it was absolutely necessary? These questions won't be answered in the foreseen future but in an information crazed world- it's funny that no one knew what was going on until now.

August 13th

Not Again!!!

In 2008, President Obama (then a candidate) promised to end the senseless war in Iraq and bring back our men and women serving in the war theater with dignity and respect. He also vowed never to repeat the disastrous withdrawal efforts that happened in Vietnam in the 1970's. As President, he kept his word.

Reality Check

Fast forward to the present day and a brand new terrorist group called *ISIS* is threatening peace in Iraq and the Middle East region; there is a power vacuum because people of certain religious fractions in power can't seem to agree on anything; the military is weak or unable to defend their citizens from this new surge of radical Islam. This is the reality of the situation.

President Obama has ordered air strikes to protect U.S. personnel and innocent civilians in the area and it seems like the targeted air strikes are working. However, there are barbarians at the gate (namely Republicans and Military Chiefs) urging the President to re-engage in Iraq. Being a veteran, I urge the President not to go back into a situation that is unwinnable.

The Way Forward

If Iraqis want to build a better society and a better life for themselves- they alone must defend and fight for their country. Their politicians must learn to work together and come to some sort of compromise on how to improve the lives of their fellow countrymen; Iraqis must tolerate one another religious beliefs. They can forge better relations with countries that want to help them and not play politics pitting one against another. That's the way forward.

We can send boots on the ground and we can bomb terrorist group until kingdom come. A better solution is if the people of Iraq are willing to take their destiny in their own hands and not wait for another radical group to seize power which will cause more heartache, misery and sorrow. The choice is theirs and theirs alone.

The Plea

Please Mr. President, despite the pressure to go in- don't do it. That's why we have Special Forces. Don't listen to the hawks. They will destroy your presidency if you let them.

The End of Racism: Volume 3

Once again in the American lexicon, racial profiling and police brutality has reared its ugly head and the nation must take notice of its legacy of injustice and bias among people of color- especially young men of African-American descent. Two recent incidents come to mind, first the death of Eric Garner by the hands of the NYPD officer who used the "choke hold" method to end his life. The other, the death of Michael Brown of Ferguson, Missouri- caused by a police officer who shot him in cold blood while his hands were up in the air. Both men were between the ages of 18 to 24 with no criminal records and unarmed. These are the facts.

In this case study, we will examine the Michael Brown incident and the outcome of the ongoing mistrust between law enforcement and the communities they protect.

Racial Disparity

The suburb of Ferguson (about 20 minutes away from the city of St. Louis) has a population of 22,000 and 67 percent of the residents are African-Americans. The city's police department has 58 members and 4 police officers are African-American. The average citizen (predominantly African American) is 2 times as likely to be searched or arrested. The numbers never lie:

- 84% Stops
- 92% Searches
- 93% Arrested

Involvement in the Community

There are no concrete reports linking the Ferguson Police Department with a legitimate community outreach program. The people in the community have a deep rooted distrust of law enforcement because most of the people who are appointed to *"protect and serve"* do not even live in that community. This lack of outreach puts a real distance between what the community "*wants*" and what law enforcement think they "*need*".

The lack of African-American representation, coupled with the militarization of a tiny police force tells us all we need to know about how the Ferguson Police Department.

Lack of Voting

The unemployment rate is at 22% so it's no wonder that the citizenry of Ferguson are disenfranchised. In the last city election, less than 13% bothered to vote and the city's Mayor ran unopposed. By the way, the Mayor of the town is a white man.

With unemployment at an alarming rate, looking for employment takes precedence over selecting who will run the city. However, if these residents voted for people of their own ilk- the outcome could have been dramatically different.

Anarchists

The violent protests are not always caused by people who actually live in that community but out of town anarchists. One can think back to the days of the 99% protest rallies and the "*not guilty*" verdict of a police officer who killed Oscar Grant. Anarchists were to be found destroying property and businesses in mostly disenfranchised neighborhoods or communities. These trust fund babies attach themselves to a cause and wreak havoc on communities.

Anarchists follow a simple pattern, when night falls they come out and cause all kinds of destruction. When night turns into day- the real community has to clean up the mess they leave behind. These anarchists are not invested in the community; they are there to destroy it.

A Reasonable Outcome

President Obama has deployed Attorney General Eric Holder to Ferguson to run an in depth investigation and to assure the citizens of Ferguson and the nation at large, that justice will be done. Given the follies and cover-ups of the Ferguson Police Department and the State of Missouri, it's time to bring in professionals who will bring objectivity and transparency.

In Conclusion

Over the last 2 years a disturbing trend has been developing in relation to race in this country. Oscar Grant, Trayvon Martin, Eric Garner, Michael Brown and the countless other black men who've been harassed only because of their color. There has always been a double standard in the United States but the recent cases of law enforcement killing young African-American men is downright appalling.

White America, just because some of you have insecurities and hold prejudges about minorities in this society doesn't give you the right to hold people of color in contempt. Have we not learned from the lesson Dr. Martin Luther King Jr. taught us, *"judge me by the content of my character"*.

Those who have power need to take a serious look about the position they are privileged to have. Those in power need to know that you are not there to serve a small fraction of the people, but to serve everyone.

August 27th

Problems or Solutions

Recently, I was involved in a roundtable discussion about the American school system. People had a lot to say about what was wrong with the system, but only a few had any real solutions to solve this pressing issue. The more the people who were solution oriented spoke up- the more cascading voices of the disenchanted drowned them out. As I took in the various points of views, I suddenly realized we couldn't seem to agree because we all weren't solution oriented.

I believe people love to bitch and moan; from commentators, to columnist, to bloggers (like myself) love to point out problems that seem so obvious.

Very rarely do we see solution based actions making front page news unless a terrorist plot is foiled.

We need to change our way of thinking. We need to be a solution oriented society for the sake of the human race. I'm personally sick and tired of lame ass excuses and rehashing of old tired grievances. What are we going to take from the lessons that history taught us? Will we continue on a foolish path or should we evaluate and come up with reasonable solutions that will benefit all.

Some of the current issues that are facing the world I believe have a very simple solution:

Israel/Palestine Conflict:

Israel should stop building new settlements in Palestine. Also, Palestinians should be allowed to work in Israel so they can earn a living wage because men or women who work are less likely to hold any grudges.

Unrest in Africa:

Major companies who are in Africa should allow people in that community to work for their companies and not hire foreign workers when the locals are able and willing. Also, elected officials should provide proper roads, schools and hospital to the masses and demand that companies who do business in the community have an obligation to support it.

Middle East: refer to Unrest in Africa
Southeast Asia: refer to Unrest in Africa
South & Central America: refer to Unrest in Africa
Eastern Europe: refer to Unrest in Africa

It seems that decision makers are willing to turn a blind eye to the solutions in favor of profit. From big corporations, NGO's, hedge fund managers and all points in between the bottom line is that maintaining the status quo is profitable.

It's not all doom and gloom because we as a collective group can change things. We have only to take a look at moral leaders like Gandhi, Dr. King and

Mother Teresa to see that solutions put into actions can change our world and history for the better. So to all you solution oriented people out there, I stand with you shouting, "WAKE UP…. AND WORK TOGETHER!!!!"

Statue of Gandhi. San Francisco, CA

September 4th

What the Hell Happened In August?

August 2014 was one of the strangest months of turmoil that I can recall in a long time. On the American landscape there was a focus on racial profiling, militarization and abuse of the citizenry by law enforcement. On the international front, an Ebola epidemic in West Africa; another Malaysian Airline flight disaster over war torn Ukraine; strife between Russia and Ukraine; battle between the Israelis and the Palestinians continues; civil war continues in Syria. To add to the chaos-the rise of an unknown terrorist group **ISIS** causing unrest in Northern Iraq and cowardly beheading 2 American journalists. What a tumultuous month!

September 16th

What is Domestic Violence?

The common definition of the term "Domestic Violence" is, "*violent or aggressive behavior within the home, typically involving the violent abuse of a spouse or partner.*" The abuse can also be verbal. Last week, the spotlight turned to that very issue involving one of the most powerful sporting leagues in America- the National Football League (NFL) and their mishandling of a domestic violence issue involving one of the most popular player in the league –Ray Rice. Now, I can rehash that ugly video footage of the incident or make the case that the powers that be in the NFL need to all step down and consider different career paths, but there is a bigger issue that needs to be addressed. What happened in the Ray Rice incident gives us the opportunity to discuss the underlying and ongoing issue of domestic violence.

Power

In most domestic violence incidents the aggressor has (or believed to have) a sense of power or dominance. Usually this attitude comes from a strong economic position or physical intimidation. The aggressor is usually the bread winner and feels the need to impose their will on the victim if they feel a sense of losing control. This same physical and psychological method was used during *American slavery*, the *"Jim Crow"* American South, the South African *Apartheid* system and by the Nazi Party against the people of Jewish descent in World War 2 (*the Holocaust*).

Learnt Behavior

The reason why the aggressor rarely feels little to no remorse is because most of the time they grew up with that sort of behavior. If someone presents a problem, beat them up to shut them up. This is learnt behavior. The parent is the first teacher of the child and if that child sees that hitting someone solves problems-then they will handle the situation the same way. As the author James Baldwin once said, *"Children have never been very good at listening to their elders, but they have never failed to imitate them."*

Conclusion

We can all blame the judiciary system and the NFL for taking the issue of domestic violence lightly, but we as a country have to look deeper at ourselves. We are a violent country and if other countries try to mess with us then they're going to get dealt with (i.e. *ISIS*). This country has a history of violence-period. The change comes within our homes and our children. In each of our homes we must set the example and tell the little ones that hitting someone that is weaker than you won't resolve problems. Only an open dialogue can help resolve this issue-the change begins with you.

This is the Beginning of the End

Recently, the American public seems to be put off by President Obama's actions on a number of issues. If I was the President, I wouldn't be worried. This has always happened to every American President entering the twilight of their presidency- the *Lame Duck* period. Critics and pundits alike will be cynical of every move that the President makes from now on. These moves are motivated to set up the narrative for the upcoming 2016 Presidential election. You know the scenario is being played out when people in his own party and the opposition distant themselves from current administration policies to set themselves up as a *"real voice for the American people"*. In every election cycle I've seen this over and over again and the American public falls for it every single time.

Reason Why Things Stay the Same

The New York Times stated that 90% of elected officials in the U.S. are white and of that number, 71% are white males. No wonder we are struck in the preverbal status quo. From the powers that be in his own party; to the obstructionist Tea Party Republicans and their Republican counterparts- the fix was in. President Obama was supposed to be a President by name only. The puppet masters were angered when he actually acted and became a President and didn't play his role like Reagan and George W. Bush did.

Short Memories

The American public has a very short memory of what happened before President Obama took office. Let me jog their memory-the world was in economic and social chaos. The President's agenda was to bring stability to the U.S. and world markets so that people can work again. Not since President Franklin D. Roosevelt has a President had to deal with so many issues on his plate at once. The U.S. and world economy is on track and the reputation of the U.S. has been restored. In a 6 year period, to do all what his administration has done is simply amazing.

The Middle East

It is naïve to think that one President can fix the ongoing issues of the Middle East. Let's just face it there will never be peace in the Middle East. President Obama's administration was trying to limit U.S. presence in the Middle East by ending the war in Iraq and wrapping up our war time operation in Afghanistan; he was ending the Bush Wars. However, new terrorist groups vying for control are popping up like chicken pox forcing the administration to take some sort of action after the beheading of two American journalists. This is a situation that the President can't win; you're damned if you don't take action against these thugs and you're damned if you refuse to do anything. This current issue has presented an opening for friends and foes to criticize the administration one way or another. This is the political cycle- the crazy season.

History

History will be kind to you Mr. President just like history was kind to Mr. Truman; Mr. Franklin Roosevelt and Mr. Lincoln. All these men were scorned by their party, their enemies and their critics. These men didn't look for the easy way out- they were shaped by their times and did what was necessary because the times demanded it. Take heart Mr. President- forget the critics and do what's right.

Artist rendition of President Obama. Jackson Square, New Orleans LA.

For What It's Worth: Volume 3

The Ebola virus scare is shedding a light on how ill prepared most American hospital facilities are to deal with this potential pandemic. Some people blame the Center for Disease Control (CDC) for lack of proper training; others blame the Republicans in Congress for eliminating some funding to the CDC to deal with problems just like this. Let's face it, no one in this country dreamt that some disease that affects West Africa would make it to our shores. It would be like the H1N1 flu scare- it will never happen- right?

With the Ebola panic at an all-time high (in the midst of mid-term election season) some Republicans in Congress are calling for President Obama to put a travel ban restriction on all effective nations. Not only is this a silly idea- it's a reactionary response to things we don't medically understand. This essay will illuminate how stupid this proposal really is.

Reason 1

There are no direct flights from Africa to the U.S. This statement bears repeating: *There are no direct flights from Africa to the U.S.* The fact of the matter is that all flights that originate in Africa go through Europe first before arriving in the U.S.

Besides, countries in West Africa have no visas to go to other neighboring West African countries. If they can't take a flight out of Liberia they will just go to the country of Mali. If people from West African countries want to come to the U.S.-they will. If you let people travel from their origin country you have a better chance of stopping them before they enter the country. This fear monger tactic is signature hallmarks of the Republican Party- incite fear to win votes.

Reason 2

If a travel ban is placed on the affected West African countries, that means no flights from Europe will ever come to the U.S. Do you realize the economic chaos that will ensue if this is allowed to happen- another potential recession. The European economy is already fragile; if a travel ban restriction is allowed it will mean that any trade between Europe and the U.S. will be hampered. In laymen terms, high prices on goods and services for everyone.

I'm surprised that the Republican Party-the so-called champions of capitalist everywhere- would come up with such a dumb idea.

Conclusion

As I stated before, no one from the World Health Organization, CDC, or the United Nations saw this coming. Everyone believed that this virus will only affect West Africa nations. Just like the hurricanes that originate from that region to take aim at the New World, Ebola slowly took shape and developed into one of the worst disease in recent times.

Not since the beginning of the HIV/AIDS epidemic have I seen such panic and misinformation flying around. If countries provide the proper funding, educate the public and allow the medical professions to do their jobs- I think we can breathe a little easier.

October 29th

Scary Things: Volume 2

In keeping with the spirit of the Halloween season-I would like to share my deepest fears with the 1Lovejoy nation. These are just a few thoughts that frighten and keep me up in the middle of the night. Without further ado, here are a few scary scenarios for this Halloween.

> A conservative and non-compassionate U.S. Supreme Court
> Ebola pandemic
> Ignorance
> Another breach in the levee system that protects New Orleans
> The build–up of the Chinese Naval Fleet
> The Pakistani government knowingly harboring terrorist(s)
> Iran actually having nuclear weapons
> The Republicans taking control of the Senate in 2015

Rupert Murdoch not being punished for the phone-hacking scandal
Tea Party Republicans
People's apathy
Racial and gender inequality
Religious and political extremists
Mormons
Fox News
Conservative Talk Radio
The collapse of the Euro Zone
H1N1 pandemic

These are just a few things to ponder. Have a Happy and safe Halloween weekend.

November 5th

Coming Soon....U.S. Government Shutdown 2015

Recently, President Obama has been thrust from crisis to crisis and because of these events has been dealing with a surge of unpopularity. It was easy for the Republican Party to ride the wave of discontentment. In the 2014 U.S. mid-term elections fear ruled the day. It was no surprise that the Republicans maintained control of the House of Representatives but now they have seized the Senate. This may not mean much at this moment but we are repeating the same pattern that occurred in 2006 (the last time the Republican Party controlled both houses in Congress). This was the time when deregulation of the financial sector was commonplace and the culture wars were at its zenith. I fear these days are coming around again.

Deregulation

On Wall Street, investors are already eying investments in the energy and equities sector. In other words, they believe that the problems in the Middle East & Africa will continue, which means that the price of oil will rise-again.

Also, most people believe that since the Republican Party will control both houses, that future legislation will benefit the financial sector (deregulation of banks). This will place an even bigger gap between the have and have-nots. In case we forget, deregulation caused the world economy to go through the worst recession in history- *The Great Recession*.

Culture Wars

Since the time of President Nixon, the culture wars are the hallmark of the Republican Party. No doubt you will see a number of legislative bills that will target individual rights and programs such as: the repeal of the Affordable Healthcare Act, repeal of gay marriage; stop funding for Planned Parenthood, stem cell research, Public television, the arts, public education and medical research funding. This is the kind of non-sense that will go on for the next 2 years. There will be no real meaningful legislation to solve the pressing issues of our day. To get their way, they will threaten to shut down the government just like in 2013 (remember how fun that was). And if history is to be our guide- it won't work.

Gridlock

For the last 6 years of his presidency, President Obama had to deal with obstructionist from friend and foe alike. His last 2 years will be no different. The Republican Party hopes to derail the President's ambitious agenda which includes immigration and tax reforms. Needless to say, that this commonsense agenda will either be stalled or pushed back. This will force the President to issue and sign *executive orders* to these initiatives. This will free up the Republican Party to stick to their mantra, *"We will say "No" to Obama on everything."*

Conclusion

If you follow this blog, I told you that the fix was in- the Republican Party had to win both the House and the Senate. The news media and big money conservative lobbyist spun it that way. They have to create a narrative for the upcoming 2016 Presidential Election. The terrorist group ISIS is on the rise, the Ebola crisis and a general fear of economic security are the perfect fear mongering issues that the Republican Party thrives on.

You've been warned, government shutdown 2015 will be coming soon.

December 8th

Hope

Awe and dismay describe the reaction to the non-indictment of New York City police officer Daniel Pantaleo for the death of Eric Garner a 42 year old African-American male killed by a fatal chokehold method that was supposed to be outlawed by NYPD. Mr. Garner's alleged offence was selling loose cigarettes which is a misdemeanor that is usually ticketed and treated just like a parking ticket. To add to this gross injustice- Mr. Garner had no loose cigarettes on his person while he was screaming the words, "*I can't breathe*" over 13 times before he expired. That's the facts.

New Hope

After the non- indictment of Officer Pantaleo, protests sprouted all across the U.S. As usual, African-Americans took their pain to the streets to illuminate this human rights issue. However, there was something a little different about this act of civil disobedience. This time I saw different hues of the American fabric, I saw Whites, Asians, people of Latin descent all standing up saying that this kind of militarizing of the police against citizens has to stop.

What impressed me the most is that young people are leading the way to organizing these ongoing demonstrations. They're using social media outlets to organize and to vocalize their displeasure.

Tea Party Mentality

What's really shocking is to hear some people think that race relations have suddenly become problematic. To them I would say," *Where have you been for the last 6 years*?" As soon as President Obama took office an ongoing campaign of fear tactics and obstructionist action was in vogue against any African-American male that was a public figure. Code words cleverly used to mask discontent by mass media and conservatives everywhere that black men (especially those in power) should be watched at all times. Remember the "Beer Summit"?

Perspective

We shouldn't be surprised by this police aggression in mostly minority neighborhoods. Some people were naïve to think that the election of the first African-American President was a new chapter in race relations in this country. Don't get me wrong, race relations have gotten a little bit better but we have so much more work to do. Remember, racism is the original and ugly sin in our country's history and we must strive to eradicate it from our future if we are to become a better nation.

Memorial of Col Shaw & 54th Regiment. The 1st African-American Army Unit in the Civil War. Boston, MA.

2015

"Our lives begin to end the day we become silent about things that matter."

— Dr. Martin Luther King Jr.

The Ghost of David Duke

It was discovered recently, that in 2002 while serving in the Louisiana Legislature Louisiana Republican Congressman Steve Scalise, attended and spoke to a white supremacist group (European-American Unity and Rights Organization). This particular group was founded by former Ku Klux Klan's (KKK) Grand Wizard and former candidate for the governorship of Louisiana-David Duke. The European-American Unity and Rights Organization group claims they seek *"Equal rights for White Americans."*

Blogger Lamar White first reported this news. Reacting to the news, Scalise the No. 3 Republican in the U.S. House of Representatives called a local news channel to give a phone interview and said:

> *"Basically if a group called me and asked me to speak, I would go and talk to them about my plans to both oppose the Stelly Plan and I was also working on eliminating slush funds," Scalise said. "So I spoke to groups. I'm not familiar with who that group was, but from what I've seen about them they don't represent what I represent. I just detest hate groups of any kind."*

Then when the national media got word of this story, Mr. Scalise's director of communication Moira Bagley Smith issued a statement saying:

> *"Throughout his career in public service, Mr. Scalise has spoken to hundreds of different groups with a broad range of viewpoints. In every case, he was building support for his policies, not the other way around. In 2002, he made himself available to anyone who wanted to hear his proposal to eliminate slush funds that wasted millions of taxpayer dollars as well as his opposition to a proposed tax increase on middle-class families. He has never been affiliated with the abhorrent group in question. The hate-fueled ignorance and intolerance that group projects is in stark contradiction to what Mr. Scalise believes and practices as a father, a husband, and a devoted Catholic."*

Then to shore up his claim that he's not a racist, he called on African-American Democratic Congressman Cedric Richmond (from New Orleans) to vouch for his character:

> "I don't view Steve as having racial challenges at all. I think that he is just a hard-working public servant that would go talk to anybody at any time, whether he agrees with their social beliefs or not"

A few days later it was discovered that Mr. Scalise while a member of the Louisiana Legislature stated *'I'm David Duke without all the baggage'*.

The Real Issue

Being Catholic and a son of Louisiana, I'm embarrassed and ashamed that this S.O.B has any association with my state. In 1991, the state was at a racial boiling point when David Duke was running for governor. Old hatred was rekindled as mistrust between the races ensued and at the end of the day, the former Grand Wizard received only 8% of overall votes. Most people moved on and reconciled their differences to build a stronger and more diverse state.

I remember the rhetoric that was used in the Duke campaign and it's not much different to what most conservatives and Tea Party Republicans use to rally their bases. The 1991 Duke Fear campaign continues to be their running mantra.

The Call to Stepdown

The KKK is a homegrown terrorist group whose doctrine is to defend the white race and to hate people of color and people who practice the religion of Judaism and Catholicism. That's the facts.

Mr. Scalise being an educated man said that he was not familiar about the group that he was speaking to at that time. If this statement is true, then the Congressman is lying or has an incompetent staff that didn't do any reasonable vetting of this organization before letting him speak to that group. In any case, Mr. Scalise needs to stepdown as the Republican Whip immediately.

After 5 years of attacking President Obama over his policies, it makes Congressman Scalise look like a crusty old white racist trying to stop the President (a black man) from doing his job. Now, when the Congressman goes to speak, every reporter will follow up with questions about his involvement with a white supremacist group in 2002.

Mr. Scalise, you lost all credibility with your colleagues, with the media, the White House and the state of Louisiana. Just do us all a favor and stepdown so the state of Louisiana can purge itself from the Ghost of David Duke once and for all.

Gordon Parks: Segregation Story. Arthur Roger Gallery. 2014 New Orleans, LA.

January 28th

#RupertsFault

On January 11th, Comedian Aziz Ansari started a meme on twitter called #RupertsFault. This meme was in response to the Australian Media Mogul's generalization of Muslims after the attack on Charlie Hebdo in Paris. On January 9th, Mr. Murdoch stated on his twitter account:

Rupert Murdoch @rupertmurdoch · Jan 9
Big jihadist danger looming everywhere from Philippines to Africa to Europe to US. Political correctness makes for denial and hypocrisy.

↰   ⇄ 3.7K   ★ 2.3K   •••

Rupert Murdoch @rupertmurdoch · Jan 9
Maybe most Moslems peaceful, but until they recognize and destroy their growing jihadist cancer they must be held responsible.

↰   ⇄ 7.1K   ★ 3.7K   •••

After seeing what Mr. Murdoch had tweeted, Mr. Ansari followed suit by writing:

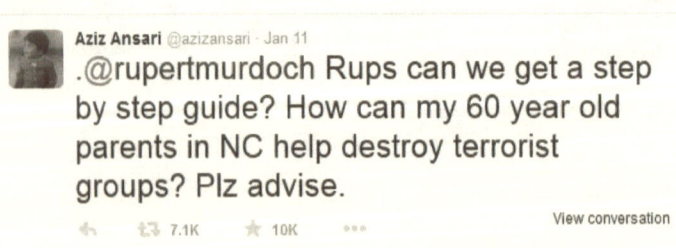

Aziz Ansari @azizansari · Jan 11
.@rupertmurdoch Rups can we get a step by step guide? How can my 60 year old parents in NC help destroy terrorist groups? Plz advise.

↰   ⇄ 7.1K   ★ 10K   •••   View conversation

Then Mr. Ansari followed up with:

Aziz Ansari @azizansari · Jan 11
.@rupertmurdoch is Christian just like Mark David Chapman who shot John Lennon. Why didn't Rupert stop it? #RupertsFault

↩   ↻ 2.8K   ★ 4.7K   •••

With these 2 tweets a meme was born. 1lovejoy nation, if you have a twitter account, let's join Mr. Ansari's revolution in stopping Mr. Murdoch and people of his ilk to think before making sweeping generalizations about Muslims or anyone who doesn't cater to his brand of social and political conservatism.

February 10th

Beware of that MOJO

A new synthetic marijuana has hit the street with the affect that is similar to heroine *"Bath Salt"*. This new drug is called *Mojo* (or Spice). The consequence of using this drug has been so deadly that in 2010, the Louisiana Legislature deemed this synthetic drug illegal.

Origins

Mojo is actually a synthetic herbal incense but someone figured out that Mojo can give you the same high as marijuana. Since this faux pot lacks the chemical THC, the person taking this product wouldn't get popped on a drug test. This pricey alternative can be found in head shops and gas stations. Most shop owners would tell you that only adults purchase this product.

The Trickle Down Effect

The more that teenagers are finding out about this drug the more they are using it. These young people think that this faux pot is harmless - how wrong they are.

The Legal Issue

This blogger has not had an opinion about the legalization of marijuana. I feel that it's a state issue but if synthetic alternatives like Mojo exist- I believe that legalizing marijuana is the way to go. Anything made in a lab dish that is not from the earth is always a bad idea to ingest into your body.

States like *Colorado* and *Washington* have shown the rest of the country how to manage and control marijuana. In the process of doing this, revenue is up and crime rates and deadly behavior due to drug uses are down.

If legalizing marijuana can get designer faux pot off the street then this blogger feels that it's the obligation of state and federal government to seriously look into this matter before some more deadly alternative comes along.

February 25th

WATCH OUT!!! You Almost Stepped In That: Volume 2

It's a shame that I have to write yet another blog post about people not picking up their dog's poop. But it seems that the situation is getting worse. Let me give you an example about how an irresponsible dog owner acted.

While taking an evening stroll, I noticed a young man on his mobile phone. The reason I was aware of his presence is because he was speaking so loudly. So, in one hand he had his mobile phone and in the other, a dog leash with a pit-bull at the other end. As the young man was talking- this dog, in the middle of the park, took one of the biggest dumps I've ever seen. Soon after the dog relieved himself, the dog owner quickly darted away like a thief in the night with no intention of picking up after his dog.

A lot of stuff bothers me but this behavior of dog owners not picking up their dog's shit drives me nuts. I will make this statement again until I'm blue in the face - you shouldn't own a dog if you can't pick up after it. Dog owners who exhibit this sort of behavior are self-centered and selfish.

The solution is simple- carry a bag at all time while walking your dog or don't own a dog at all.

March 25th

The Cancer Event

Recently, I attended a charity event that had willing participates shave their hair to raise money to fight the ongoing battle against cancer. The day appeared to be a success. However, there was one activity that was happening that seemed a little peculiar- people smoking cigarettes.

There were participates smoking before their hair was shaved hair off, parents smoking in front of their children and a group of friends smoking at a nearby table- I think you get the picture. This blogger has no claim to be a medical expert but isn't smoking cigarettes one of the leading causes of contracting cancer.

It's a shame that the people who are willing the shave their hair to raise money to fight against cancer could be the same people who may need the assistance of a cancer organization in the near future.

April 8th

Social Terrorist

Recently at a comedy show in Wilmington, Delaware, comedian Hannibal Buress stopped a heckler in their tracks by calling that person a "Social Terrorist" for destroying the mood in the room. The audience laughed with delight with this accurate description of the event.

The Urban Dictionary has several definitions of this term: Here is the best description by *StockCasa* on August 25 2011;

"People who are always nice when in a group or at work or school and always shaking hands and smiling. When they get home they start their assaults on mankind via blogs, posts, and other internet media outlets with cursing, racial indignation, name calling and general harassment of anyone and everyone. Only to return to work, school, etc. smiling and maintaining their normal *sleeper cell* persona."

With the ongoing anti-bullying campaign the term *'Social Terrorist'* will be the new meme of 2015. People are tired of spending money on a concert or a sporting event just to have irritating people ruin the mood for everyone. This sort of behavior is not cute or amusing- it just plain sucks.

Thank you so much Mr. Buress, for exposing rude people for what they are- *'Social Terrorist's'*.

April 22nd

A Stagnant Economy

On a recent episode of Fareed Zakaria's GPS, former Treasury Secretary Larry Summers pointed out that the U.S. economy is back on track. However, the economy will remain stagnant if private investors stay away from the stock market. Mr. Summers believes that with historically low interest rates it's the right time to invest in stocks and take out loans to really energize the markets.

Mr. Summer is right –in theory. In reality, the public at large doesn't trust bankers and least of all the people who run Wall Street. With the worst economic disaster since the great recession that looms in our collective memories- how can anyone put their trust and money in Wall Street? In other words, a lack of trust of financial institutions still exists.

Getting a Loan

If you ask Mr. and Mrs. John Q. Public, they will tell you that taking a loan with the any financial institution is damn near impossible. The endless amount of paperwork and the delving into one's personal life makes the average person feel like they're being vetted to become the Secretary of the Treasury. In the meantime, the people and businesses that ran the world economy to ground have an open line of credit- no questions asked.

If you see this sort of behavior happening over and over again, would you feel confident in investing your money?

Reality Check

It will be a long time until people feel confident about financial institutions. The trust is lost. People are still feeling the pain that Wall Street inflicted on millions of families around the globe. The only way people are going to invest in the market again is if a tighter rein is put on Stock Brokers and Hedge Fund managers. This mean that the SEC (Securities and Exchange Commission) needs to do their job and regulate these fat cats on Wall Street instead of being buddies with them.

If people feel that the SEC is doing their jobs and if the U.S. Congress issues tighter regulation and oversight on financial institutions, then confidence might be restored for the average investor.

When trust returns, the U.S. economy will be in a stronger position. So financial Institutions need to find a new way to re-establish a bond with their clients if everyone is to prosper.

Wall Street. New York, NY

May 13th

About Baltimore

I wanted all the noise to stop and the non-stop coverage to end before making any commentary about the events that took place in Baltimore, Maryland over the senseless death of Freddie Gray. This marks the latest incident involving police officer(s) taking the life of yet another unarmed, innocent African-American male which led to yet another widespread protest and again brought attention to this ongoing problem.

This post is not going to be a rant about the current criminal justice system, the need for police reform or a call for more proactive community involvement. This post is about Baltimore Orioles Executive Vice President John Angelos (son of majority owner Peter Angelos) and his twitter account.

When the Mayor and Police Department of Baltimore placed a curfew on the city, the baseball team was asked to comply to insure the safety of their fans. The baseball club had no problem and followed the order. However, something remarkable happened when Mr. John Angelos tweeted about the problems in Baltimore and our society at-large. Here are his tweets that were edited for cohesion:

> *"Brett, speaking only for myself, I agree with your point that the principle of peaceful, non-violent protest and the observance of the rule of law is of utmost importance in any society. MLK, Gandhi, Mandela, and all great opposition leaders throughout history have always preached this precept. Further, it is critical that in any democracy investigation must be completed and due process must be honored before any government or police members are judged responsible.*
>
> *That said, my greater source of personal concern, outrage and sympathy beyond this particular case is focused neither upon one night's property damage nor upon the acts, but is focused rather upon the past four-decade period during which an American political elite have shipped middle class and working class jobs away from Baltimore and cities and towns around the U.S. to third-world dictatorships like China and others, plunged tens of millions*

of good hard-working Americans into economic devastation, and then followed that action around the nation by diminishing every American's civil rights protections in order to control an unfairly impoverished population living under an ever-declining standard of living and suffering at the butt end of an ever-more militarized and aggressive surveillance state.

The innocent working families of all backgrounds whose lives and dreams have been cut short by excessive violence, surveillance, and other abuses of the Bill of Rights by government pay the true price, an ultimate price, and one that far exceeds the importance of any kids' game played tonight, or ever, at Camden Yards. We need to keep in mind people are suffering and dying around the U.S., and while we are thankful no one was injured at Camden Yards, there is a far bigger picture for poor Americans in Baltimore and everywhere who don't have jobs and are losing economic civil and legal rights, and this makes inconvenience at a ball game irrelevant in light of the needless suffering government is inflicting upon ordinary Americans."

Mr. John Angelos should be heralded for his bold statements about race, employment, poverty and lack of opportunity for some. He is the only affluent person of note that has had the courage to speak about the real problems facing Baltimore and our country. I truly hope the powers that be (and all of us) heed his message sooner rather than later.

The Week that Changed America

In the ever changing American narrative real change emerged in the last week of June. The Supreme Court of the United States handed down 2 rulings that will forever transform the way Americans view themselves. First, the court upheld the Affordable Care Act (Obamacare) that allows subsidies to be used to aid people who can't afford healthcare in all 50 states. Secondly, the court also ruled that same-sex marriage will be recognized in all 50 states. This opens the door for people of the same gender who wish to wed as they will have all the legal rights afforded to them, the same as a traditional married couple.

With these two rulings, a seismic shift in the culture wars and patient's rights has been affirmed by the highest court in the land and reflects the ever involving attitude in our country's attempt to be *a more perfect union*'.

However, as transformative as those 2 rulings are, the real change came when a lone wolf white supremacist shot and killed 9 people in a church in Charleston, South Carolina during a bible study class. When this disturbed young man was captured and faced the families of the deceased, the families showed nobility and compassion by choosing to forgive this man for his misguided hate.

Moreover, when President Obama gave his eulogy for one of the Emanuel 9, he called for the removal of the Confederate flag and called on the nation (and the world) to have the same grace that was displayed by the Emanuel 9 families. Then the President ended the eulogy by singing the spiritual "Amazing Grace". The President's powerful speech about race and the symbolic meaning of the Confederate flag illuminated the horrible memories of oppression and subjugation suffered under this symbol. As people hearts opened, a number of Southern states and businesses finally started the process of removing this symbol of Ole' Dixie.

The last week in June will transform this country for years to come. We can (for now) say that America found its' humanity when the Supreme Court upheld the key provision of The Affordable Care Act; showed empathy with the same-sex marriage ruling and ended the final chapter in the American Civil War by removing the symbol of a bygone era.

On this 239th, 4th of July weekend, we have something to truly celebrate - the ability to change and see the error of our ways.

Christopher Columbus statue. Coit Tower Telegraph Hill. San Francisco, California

July 4th

Goodbye Rupert

Dear Rupert,

I heard your son James has taken over your Fox Empire. Is it true? Well, I never thought I'd see the day that you would not be involved in an upcoming U.S. Presidential election having your right wing minions spreading the doctrine of supply-side economics and cutting taxes for the rich. I just can't believe it. You must be getting old for this sort of thing.

Well, in any case, it's good to see you departing from the world stage. I would be naïve to think you're going to leave the scene completely. I'm sure you're still looking for that perfect handpicked Republican candidate that your Fox news cable network seems to put out every week. I don't think you're going to be happy with the 2016 selections. So leave while you're ahead.

It appears that your son James is more level headed and fair minded about his worldviews. He seems to be business minded and not interested in being a puppet master (I hope).

So, farewell to you Rupert, I hope you go back down under and stay there. Your right-wing vile and influence has polarized communities and lined your pockets. I hope you're proud about what you've done. Given your track record- you probably are.

Regards,

1lovejoy

p.s. My job is done

Epilogue

As I stated before, I wrote the 1lovejoy blog to chronicle the presidency of Barack Obama. Along the way I noticed agendas and added my own personal observations to give perspective to the chain of human events. After reading some of these entries one might feel a bit pessimistic about the world around us. However, I take a different view as I feel that the world should be encouraged by the engagement of young people being socially active in our society.

Someone once said *"Freedom isn't Free"* and not taking a more active role in the society one lives in will not change anything. Throughout history there are many examples of people not doing anything and later on being oppressed by a government or rules they didn't want to live by. The current example is the City of Ferguson, Missouri. With the death of Michael Brown, that community was awakened from their apathy about police abuse and their government. Now, that community is getting involved making their voice heard in the media and the voting booth. It was unfortunate that Mr. Brown lost his life but that event stirred something up in people that a fundamental change needed to happen and that the status quo was no longer acceptable.

With the twilight of the Obama presidency, I feel that these entries summed up what was happening in this era - from the economic recovery; to outbreaks of diseases; to racial politics; to worldwide protest; to the resiliency of the human spirit. I hope by reading these entries that you take away some sense that you and I and everyone in this world are all connected in some small way. So ends the lesson.

J.C. Phillips is an Iraq War Veteran, Political Researcher/Organizer, turned writer/blogger. He lives in New Orleans with his wife. This book is his first endeavor.

2011

1. "Raped In Libya" Article and video by Mark Phillips from CBS News
2. "It's the End of the World...Again" Reporter Mike Sugarman from CBS 5 News in San Francisco.
3. "Death to Trickle-Down Economics!"; Tax the Rich! by David Cay Johnston
4. "Introducing The Viagra Condom"; "Could a New Viagra Condom Encourage Safe Sex" by Meredith Melnick for Time.com
5. "The End of the World Didn't Happen... Now What?;" "Despite Careful Calculations, the World Does Not End" by Jesse McKinley from *The New York Times.com*
6. "Stop!! No Saggy Pants Allowed" ; *"Airline keeps saggy pants on the ground* "by Dan Schreiber from *The San Francisco Examiner*
7. "Check Out My Index Finger!!!" *"Penis Size: It May be written in the Length of His Fingers"* by Maia Szalavitz for Time.com ; Judging penis size by comparing index, ring finger by Thomas H. Maugh II for Los Angeles Times; Actual Study by Research Team for Asian Journal of Andrology
8. "Carpe Diem" ; *Troubles That Money Can't Dispel* by David Carr for New York Times.com ; *Phone Hacking: The News international denials*-video by guardian.co.uk
9. "What Happened to Sean Hoare?" ; *Whistle-Blower in Phone-Hacking Case Reportly Found Dead* by Robert Mackey for New York Times.com ; Sean Hoare postmortem results confirm death not suspicious by Paul Lewis for guardian.co.uk
10. "Blame Yourself America!!"; S&P official defend US credit downgraded by Martin Crutsinger for The Associated Press
11. "Muammar Hearts Leezza" ; *Gaddafi Loves Condi: Libyan Dictator Kept Photos of former Secretary of State* by Megan Gibson of Time.com
12. "Can Ecstasy Cure Cancer?" ; *Modified ecstasy attack blood cancers* by James Gallagher for BBC News
13. "99 Percent" ; Official Website for the Occupy Wall Street http://occupywallst.org/ ; Unions endorse, will join Occupy Wall Street Protest by Jason Kessler & Michael Martinez for CNN.com
14. "What Were Steve Jobs' Last Words?" ; With Time Running Short, Jobs Managed His Farewells by Julie Bosman, Quentin Hardy, Claire Cain

Miller and Evelyn M. Rusli for New York Times.com ; Too Soon? Sony Acquires Rights to Steve Jobs Biopics by Glen Levy for Time.com

15. "What Were Steve Jobs Last Words? : Volume 2" ; Steve Jobs' Sister Reveals His Last Words in Eulogy. By Doug Aamoth for Time.com

16. "Occupy Equals Financiers"; Occupy San Francisco Starts Its Own Credit Union by Martha White for Time.com ; Occupy Shocker: A Realistic, Actionable Idea by David Weidner for Wall Street Journal.com ; Occupy San Francisco Unveil People's Reserve Credit Union by SF Occupy on Facebook

17. "An Offer For Robert Reich"; Robert Reich's blog by robertreich.org

2012

1. "Jim Crow All Over Again: The America's Cup" ; *Capitalizing On The Auld Mug"* by Rebecca Bowe for The Guardian

2. "The Great Migration Back to the South" ; For New Life, Blacks in City Head To South by Dan Bilefsky for New York Times.com ; The Great Migration (African-Americans) for Wikipedia.com

3. "The Importance of the Separation of Church and State" ; Rick Santorum regrets "throw-up" remark about John Kennedy stance on church-state divide by Shria Schoenberg for Boston.com ; Separation of church and state by Wikipedia

4. "Limbaugh's Fluke" ; Limbaugh Apologizes for Attack on Student in Birth Control Furor by Brian Stelter for New York Times.com

5. "Strip Search Everyone" ; Supreme Court Ruling Allows Strip-Searches for Any Arrest by Adam Liptak for New York Tmes.com

6. "Nazis In Congress" ; Nazi Party Gets First Lobbyist on Capitol Hill by Alyssa Newcomb for abcnews.go.com ; Nazis Get Their Own Lobbyist by Robert Schlesinger for usnews.com ; The American Nazi Party has registered a lobbyist in Congress by Peter Bella for washingtontimes.com

7. "The Great Student Loan Debt Debate" ; Student Loan Interest Rates Loom as Political Battle by Tamar Lewin for New York Times.com

8. "In Yo' Face (book), Saverin" ; Dem senators introduce bill to punish Facebook co-founder Eduardo Saverin by Stephanie Condon for cbsnews.com

9. "Defend New Orleans: Volume 2" ; A Doomed Romance with a New Orleans Newspaper by David Carr for New York Times.com

10. "It's Official... No One Likes Mitt Romney" ; Speaker Boehner: 'The American People Probably Aren't Going To Fall In Love With Mitt Romney' by Frances Martel for mediaite.com

2013

1. The Trouble with Donations and NPO's ; U.S. victims of mass shooting seek control over donations By: Daniel Trotta for reuters.com
2. Comfortable In His Own Skin ; *Why NBA center Jason Collins is coming out now?* By Jason Collins with Franz Lidz for si.com
3. Stop and Frisk: Ruled Unconstitutional ; *Two Powerful Signals of a Major Shift on Crime* by Charlie Savage & Erica Goode for nyt.com

2014

1. America's New Slavery System: Prison ; *Study: Record Number of U.S. Convicts cleared in 2013* by BBC News
2. The Mayans Were Almost Right ; Earth survived near-miss from 2012 solar storm: NASA by AFP

2015

1. The Ghost of David Duke ; "Scalise admits to speaking to white supremacist group" by Wynton Yates for wwltv.com
2. #RupertsFault ; *"Aziz Ansari Launches' # RupertFault 'to Sarcastically Blame Rupert Murdoch for Everything"* by Alex Heigl for *People.com*

www.ingramcontent.com/pod-product-compliance
Lightning Source LLC
Chambersburg PA
CBHW050442290526
45786CB00006B/2123